A Portrait of a Healthy Church

An Exposition of
1 Thessalonians

Malcolm Webber

Published by:

Strategic Press
Division of Strategic Global Assistance, Inc.
513 S. Main St. Suite 2
Elkhart, IN 46516
U.S.A.

Toll free: 1-844-532-3371 (1-844-LEADER1)

www.sgai.org

Our secure online bookstore: www.StrategicPress.org

Copyright © 2020 Malcolm Webber
ISBN: 9781888810967

All Scripture references are from the English Standard Version of the Bible, unless otherwise noted.

Printed in the United States of America

Contents

Contents 3

Introduction 5

A Brief Summary of the Healthy Church Model 9

A Chronology of Events in Thessalonica 21

Chapter 1 25
   1:1 The Greeting 25
   1:2-3 Thanksgiving for the Thessalonians 31
   1:4-10 The Establishing of the Thessalonian Church 37

Chapter 2 49
   2:1-12 Paul's Ministry in Thessalonica 49
   2:13-16 The Thessalonians' Reception of the Gospel 67
   2:17-20 Paul's Longing for the Thessalonians 73

Chapter 3 77
   3:1-5 The Sending of Timothy 77
   3:6-13 Timothy's Report and Paul's Response and Prayer . . 84

Chapter 4 93
    4:1-8 Sexual Purity 93
    4:9-12 Brotherly Love and Personal Responsibility 101
    4:13-18 Believers Who Have Died 106

Chapter 5 115
    5:1-3 The Day of the Lord and the Unbelievers 115
    5:4-11 The Day of the Lord and the Believers 118
    5:12-13 Leaders in the Church 125
    5:14-18 Exhortations Toward Each Other and Toward God 132
    5:19-22 The Gifts of the Holy Spirit 136
    5:23-24 God's Empowering 139
    5:25-28 Final Instructions and Blessing 143

1 Thessalonians and the Healthy Church Model 147
    The Goal of Church Life 147
    The Process of Church Life 151

Introduction

The Thessalonian church was a healthy church.

> ... *you became an example to all the believers in Macedonia and in Achaia. For not only has the Word of the Lord sounded forth from you in Macedonia and Achaia, but your faith in God has gone forth everywhere, so that we need not say anything. (1 Thess. 1:7-8)*

Moreover, it was healthy a short time after being planted.

How did this happen? What were the key elements that went into this?

In 1 Thessalonians Paul tells us how he did this. He shows us in this rich and practical letter how he nurtured a culture of life and health.

This exposition will study the letter, verse by verse, through the lens of the Healthy Church Model.[1]

The Thessalonian Church shows us that:

- It is possible for health to be achieved by a church. The Thessalonians were "an example to all the believers in Macedonia and in Achaia" (1 Thess. 1:7). Sometimes we feel helpless and hopeless when we look at the condition of many churches and we give up and settle for less than God's highest. But health is possible!

---

[1] Please see *Building Healthy Churches* by Malcolm Webber for a complete study of this model.

- Health can be achieved quickly. Paul had only been with them for a short time. We don't know exactly how long he was there. Acts 17:2 speaks of Paul speaking at the synagogue on "three Sabbath days," but the fact that the Philippians sent him financial help two times (Phil. 4:16) indicates a longer stay – perhaps a couple of months or so. What did Paul do in that short time to establish such profound and enduring life? That is what we will study in this book.
- A healthy church will have powerful ministry impact. This church had significant impact across two provinces (1 Thess. 1:8). A healthy church is not merely healthy for its own sake. God has called us to impact our communities and nations!
- Health in a church can be achieved with a minimum of outside influence when dependence on the Holy Spirit is fostered. Paul was there for only a few months initially (Acts 17:1-10), and Timothy was there briefly later (1 Thess. 3:2). Thus, there was not much outside help for these new believers. Church planting and church building is the work of the Holy Spirit. Paul and his team trusted in the Holy Spirit to do the work and He did it well!
- "Health" does not mean "perfection." Paul addresses problems in this same letter (e.g., 1 Thess. 4:1-8). The Thessalonian church was not perfect. Our goal must be realistic.

In short, 1 Thessalonians shows us what a healthy church is and how it is built.

My hope for this exposition is that it will provide a practical roadmap for those who plant and lead churches.

As you read this exposition, please go slowly. This will help you to dig deeply into Paul's words and the spiritual reality of New Testament church life.

Much of the writing today on churches focuses on structure, strategy, programs and systems. Our focus here will not be on techniques but on the *life* of the leaders and the churches they lead. If we can get the life right, then, by God's grace, the right structure will follow – and the Church will be the beautiful Bride, the glorious Temple and the mature Body that Jesus died for and will soon return for!

Malcolm Webber, Ph.D.
June 2020

A Brief Summary of the Healthy Church Model

The Healthy Church Model gives us a simple but robust foundation for building a healthy and unified church. These are the core elements of the model:

Building His Church is the central thing God is doing on the earth.

Jesus said, "On this Rock, I will build My Church." (Matt. 16:13-19) The revelation of the Person and purpose of Jesus Christ is the Foundation on which Jesus will build His Church. This shows us the centrality of the Church in the purpose of God. It's not that God has many purposes, and this is merely one of them. This is the core purpose of God, and the purpose for which Jesus came. There are many good things we could do, but God has called us to the highest: the building of His Temple, the preparation of His Bride, the equipping and maturing of His Body. Our goal is the building of His Church.

A healthy church is one in which every member is functioning properly.

In the New Testament, the Church is compared to the human body (1 Cor. 12; Eph. 4). When a part of someone's body is not functioning properly, that person is, by definition, "sick" or "unhealthy." Thus, a simple definition of a "healthy" human body is one in which every member is functioning properly. It is the same with a healthy church. Paul says, "From Him [Christ] the whole Body, joined and held together by every supporting ligament, grows and builds itself up in love, as each part does its work." (Eph. 4:16) If every member functions properly then the local church will be healthy and fulfill God's purposes.

When the people do the ministry work the church is built up.

It is vital that we understand Paul's words in Ephesians 4:11-12: "And He gave the [leaders] to equip the saints for the work of ministry, for building up the Body of Christ …" This is sometimes (incorrectly) understood as: the leaders equip the people, the leaders do the work of the ministry, and the leaders build up the Body of Christ. And the rest of the people in the church are seen as needy objects of the leaders' ministries.

In reality, Paul said: the leaders equip the people. Then the people do the work of the ministry which, in turn, is what builds up the Body of Christ. It is not the leaders who build up the Body of Christ; it is the people! The Church will *only* be built and come to maturity when the people function properly – when the people act.

The role of the leaders is to equip the people, build leaders, shape culture, and create an environment for the people to do the work of the ministry.

A leader's primary attention must not be on personally doing the ministry work, but on building the people to do the ministry work. This is not to suggest that church leaders should never do any direct ministry work themselves. Jesus did ministry work, but, most importantly, He equipped His disciples and they acted and proceeded to build the Church all over the world.

Jesus integrated the two – ministry work and equipping. Every time Jesus did ministry work, He equipped His disciples through it. His focus was building people and the ministry work provided the rich context and diverse opportunities to do so. There is no better way to equip people than in the midst of the ministry work.

To "equip" the people means to do whatever is necessary to nurture a daily life and culture in which every member functions properly.

Paul uses the word "equip" in Ephesians 4:12 to express that the church leaders are to *do whatever is necessary to nurture a daily life and culture in which every member functions properly*. This includes practical teaching, but it's much bigger than that. "Equip" includes:

- Creating a culture in which every member functions. "Culture" means shared beliefs, values, attitudes, actions, language.
- Personally building and empowering leaders who will nurture this culture across the life of the church.
- Envisioning and providing opportunities for people to function.
- Designing and implementing the necessary "spiritual infrastructure" (organization, administration, systems, resources, learning, evaluation, prayer, etc.) to support the people as they act and to ensure that all the various facets of church life work well together.

In summary, it's the people who do the work of the ministry and build up the Body of Christ, and the role of the leaders is to equip the people to do that – basically to do everything necessary to make that happen. That is what the leaders must do. Their primary attention must not be on personally doing the ministry work, but on building the people to do the ministry work.

Thus, the leaders are not called merely to *run programs* but to *build people*. This is a profound paradigm shift for many believers and churches. It is a shift away from a *program* mentality to a *people* mentality. It is a shift from *logistics* to *life*.

Here is how to evaluate your own personal focus as a leader. Ask the question: Over the last month how much time did I spend running programs (administration, logistics, etc.) and how much time did I personally spend investing in people's lives? In the Great Commission, Jesus did not say, "Go and start programs." His commandment was, "Go and make disciples" – build people's lives!

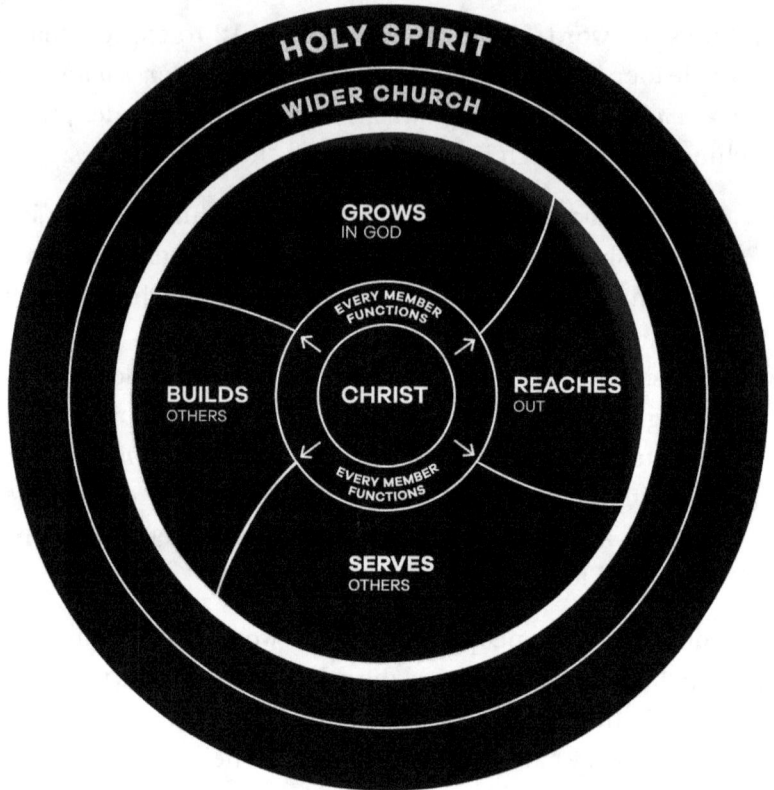

A healthy church is one in which every member grows in God, serves others, builds others and reaches out.

For a church to be healthy it must have all four facets (Eph. 4:15). Of course, churches will have seasons of special emphasis on one or another of these. However, over time, all four must be strongly built. And all four must come from life – the indwelling life of Christ in each believer's life (John 15:4-5). Our union with Christ is expressed in these four practical ways. Through these, every member and every church will fulfill both the two Great Commandments (Matt. 22:37-40, Grows in God and Serves Others) and the twofold Great Commission (Matt. 28:19-20, Builds Others and Reaches Out).

A healthy church will have a healthy relationship with other churches and with the broader Body of Christ.

Like the various members of a healthy human body (1 Cor. 12), the early churches were individually strong but they were not isolated or independent. Neither were they dependent on one another; instead there was a healthy interdependence.

Fundamentally, the overarching vision of every local church should be essentially the same.

All churches are called to the same broad vision that God gives us in Ephesians 4:11-16. It is true that some churches will have a particular capacity in a certain focused area (e.g., teaching or evangelism). But often that will revolve around the focus and special abilities of a certain highly gifted leader. Moreover, churches with a big emphasis on one or a few things are sometimes out of balance and the rest of the church's life is neglected.

Generally speaking, each local church should not try to be a special church with a unique calling. That idea came from the corporate world, in which one company tries to have a unique vision and market in order to gain a competitive advantage over other companies – this is certainly appropriate in the business world. However, there simply is no biblical support for such an idea for local churches.

The single strategy to build healthy churches is to build people's lives – to build leaders and to build everyone across the life of the church.

To use Jesus' words: "Make disciples." To use Paul's words: "Equip God's people." The core strategy of every local church must be to build leaders and to build everyone.

It is through the Four Dynamics of Transformation that the leaders nurture the life of every member functioning. "Equip" means the four dynamics.

The Four Dynamics of Transformation (4Ds) give us a very clear and practical description of exactly how this equipping occurs! It is through the four dynamics that a healthy church is built.

- Spiritual Dynamics: The Transforming Power of the Holy Spirit
- Relational Dynamics: The Transforming Power of Relationships
- Experiential Dynamics: The Transforming Power of Doing
- Instructional Dynamics: The Transforming Power of the Word of God

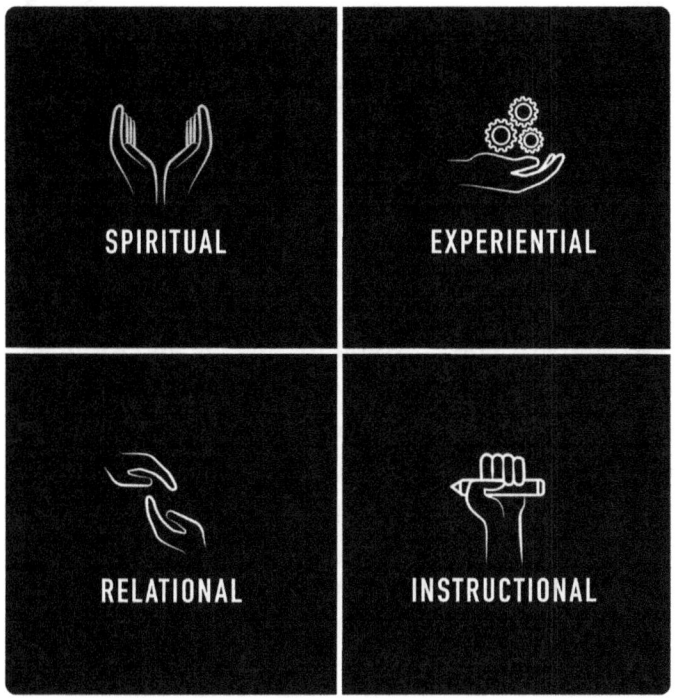

Every church in the New Testament was planted and nurtured using all four dynamics.

The apostles created a very rich environment to nurture life and to build the church – in every church in the New Testament. It was a culture of connecting with God in prayer, praise and worship, serving one another, giving, reaching out to the lost, time in the Word, fellowship with one another, and spiritual exercises (Acts 2:42-47).

The example of the Thessalonian church is dramatic. Paul spent only a short time there establishing the church (Acts 17:2) before he was sent away in the midst of fierce persecution. Yet, not long after, he writes that they're doing so well that they have become "a model to all the believers in Macedonia and Achaia" and that their "faith in God has become known everywhere" (1 Thess. 1:8)!

What did Paul do in that short time to establish such profound and enduring life? He used the four dynamics (1 Thess. 1:5-8)!

The role of the fivefold ministries (Eph. 4:11-12) is not just to do the ministry work themselves, but their primary role is to build people and nurture culture.

- **Apostle** – gives overall leadership to the church. The apostle is the general contractor ("wise master builder" – 1 Cor. 3:10) who sees how all the parts go together in a unified, productive way, and gives broad vision for change and for health. He is responsible for the total work, and gives overall direction, leadership, design and strategy.
- **Prophet** – connects people with God so that we love God, worship God, serve God, know God, depend on God, put God first. "Grows in God."
- **Pastor/Shepherd** – connects people with others in the church so that we love and serve one another. "Serves others."
- **Teacher** – connects people with truth so that we all learn and grow. "Builds others."
- **Evangelist** – connects people with passion for the lost so that we reach out. "Reaches out."

We should think of the fivefold ministries not only as formal ministry "offices" but also as roles in the life of every local church.

In the New Testament there are men and women who functioned in each of these offices (Peter was an apostle, Philip an evangelist, etc.) Moreover, there are certainly men and women today who function in each of these offices. Yet there are also many men and women who perform these *kinds* of roles in the normal daily life of a church without having the specific office.

For example, while there are some "Evangelists" in the church today, there are far more people who are "evangelistic" in their giftings and callings. If we think this way, then the door is open for almost every local church to have all five of these kinds of ministry at work.

There are potentially many legitimate forms of local church government. Moreover, what's appropriate in a certain context can change over time.

The New Testament writers had plenty of opportunity to lay out a detailed, systematic plan for church government. However, they carefully avoided doing this. In the entire book of Acts, for example, Luke never once gives specific details regarding the government of the churches at Jerusalem or Antioch. In his broad address to church leaders in 1 Peter 5:1-4, Peter (like other New Testament writers) does not promote or even define one particular and precisely detailed system of church government.

The exact form of government may vary from place to place and from time to time according to many factors, like size, culture, age, stability and maturity. The design of the actual form of church government in each case in the New Testament was the responsibility of wise church planters and leaders under the direction of the Holy Spirit (1 Cor. 3:10).

Structure must always come from life and must always serve to support life.

In church life, as the church grows and matures, the visionary leadership and new directions will create the need for particular governing and administrative structures. Structure comes from life.

These structures, in turn, are essential to protect and facilitate the life and work of the church and enable the church to continue to grow in both size and maturity. Structure serves life.

Here are some key observations regarding structure:

- The particular structure that is needed changes as the church grows and matures.
- You should have no more structure than what the life actually requires.
- At the point that your structure gets in the way of life it must be changed or eliminated, or else you will end up with the life of the church serving the structure!
- Focus on life, not structure! Let the structure come naturally. In reality, life comes first – always!

Our goal is a "Healthy Church" and not a "Perfect Church"!

Perfection is a hard task master. It is unachievable and if you pursue it, you will drive yourself and others. Your church will never be perfect, but it can be healthy!

The Healthy Church Model presents five major paradigm shifts.

These five paradigm shifts are:

Traditional Paradigm	New Testament Paradigm
1. Who builds the church?	
The leaders do the ministry work and the church is built up. The leaders build the church.	The people do the ministry work and the church is built up. The people build the church.
2. What is the role of the people of God?	
The people are needy objects and passive recipients of the leader's ministry.	The people actively function in the work of the ministry.
3. What is the role of the leader?	
The role of the leader is to do all the work of the ministry.	The role of the leader is to equip the people, build leaders, shape culture, and create an environment for the people to do the work of the ministry.
4. Where and when does "church" occur?	
"Church" occurs in a building on Sunday morning.	"Church" occurs in the homes, workplaces and lives of God's people, all week long (Acts 2:42-47).
5. How is a healthy church built?	
Run effective ministry programs.	Build people.

Throughout this exposition, we will note these various characteristics present in the Thessalonian church.

In particular, we will use the "Four Dynamics" Model to illustrate how the church was initially planted and then subsequently built. When we note Paul's use of the Instructional Dynamic we'll pay special attention to the content of his teaching, since he was intentional about the kind of things necessary to teach a new church.

A Chronology of Events in Thessalonica

Paul came to Macedonia in response to a direct revelation from God (Acts 16:9-10). After establishing a church in Philippi (Acts 16:11-40; 1 Thess. 2:2), he traveled to Thessalonica, the Macedonian capital. Paul's initial ministry in Thessalonica is described in Acts 17:1-9. He was in Thessalonica in the year ad 50 or 51.

Paul went to a synagogue in Thessalonica and preached there for three successive Sabbaths. Some Jews and Greeks, and particularly some of the prominent women, believed his teaching about Jesus as the Messiah and joined him (Acts 17:4).

It's very likely that Paul's stay there was longer than three weeks. Luke specifically mentions three weeks of teaching in the synagogue (Acts 17:2) but that does not limit Paul's stay to only that time frame. Other considerations suggest that Paul spent a few months there:

- There was a large number of Gentile converts in the city (1 Thess. 1:9).
- Paul worked to support himself (2 Thess. 3:8).
- The Philippian church sent financial aid to him several times when he was in Thessalonica (Phil. 4:16).
- He taught many things during this stay, as we will see throughout the letter.

Paul's success provoked jealously among the Jews, who started a riot and went looking for Paul and his team (Acts 17:5). Not finding them, they dragged Jason (Paul's host) and some of the believers before the city authorities, charging them with disloyalty to Caesar (Acts 17:6-7). Jason gave some money as security to those authorities (Acts 17:9), possibly guaranteeing that Paul's preaching would not cause any further trouble.

The young Thessalonian church then immediately sent Paul away by night to Berea where his ministry had a very positive reception (Acts 17:11-12). The Thessalonian Jews heard about his successful work in Berea and followed him there to stir up more trouble (Acts

17:13). Immediately he was sent away from Berea, leaving Silas and Timothy there, and traveled to Athens (Acts 17:14).

While in Athens he sent word to Silas and Timothy (by the Berean believers who had traveled with him), requesting that they come to him in Athens as soon as possible (Acts 17:15). Apparently Timothy and Silas did so. Then, from Athens, they sent Timothy to Thessalonica to see how the believers were doing and to encourage them. Silas also returned to Macedonia around the same time, perhaps to check on the Philippian church. Silas and then Timothy both returned from Macedonia to join Paul in Corinth where he had gone after Athens (Acts 18:1, 5), bringing a very positive report about the Thessalonian believers (1 Thess. 3:2, 6).

Immediately upon receiving this report (1 Thess. 3:6), while in Corinth, Paul wrote his first letter to the Thessalonians.[2]

Apparently, there was subsequent communication between Paul and the Thessalonians which led to Paul writing a second letter to address various ongoing issues. Paul wrote 2 Thessalonians not very long after the first letter, probably also from Corinth. Silas and Timothy were still with him (2 Thess. 1:1).

Paul tried to visit the Thessalonian church numerous times but was not able to (1 Thess. 2:18), until several years later (Acts 20:1-2).

---

[2] Some scholars believe that 1 Thessalonians was written by Paul from Athens very soon after his initial departure from Macedonia.

Chapter 1

1:1 THE GREETING

1 Paul, Silvanus, and Timothy, To the church of the Thessalonians in God the Father and the Lord Jesus Christ: Grace to you and peace.

Paul, Silvanus, and Timothy

Timothy and Silas (Silvanus) were with Paul when he planted the church. Silas is specifically named as being with Paul (Acts 17:4); presumably Timothy was also there. Paul left them both in Berea when he went to Athens (Acts 17:14). From Athens he called for them to come to him (Acts 17:15), and when he was in Corinth they arrived (Acts 18:5) bringing a very positive report about the Thessalonians (1 Thess. 3:2, 6).

Silas and Timothy are with him now in Corinth as he writes this letter. In the letter, he constantly uses the words "we," "our," "us."

> **Relational Dynamic:** Paul, the great apostle, thought, spoke and acted in the context of a community. He modeled accountability and healthy interdependence between team members. He was not a big, superstar leader whom everyone else served. Spiritually, he was a "family man."

Paul does not mention his apostolic office in the greeting. In other, more corrective and urgent letters, he explicitly affirms his apostolic authority (e.g., Galatians). But it's not necessary here. Paul is their spiritual father and is fully received as their spiritual father.

In 1 Thessalonians 2:6 he speaks of himself, Silas and Timothy as being "apostles of Christ," in the context of their *not* having made legitimate apostolic "demands."

> **Relational Dynamic:** Paul sought to reduce the "power distance" between himself and the people of God, always treating them as "brethren." He only affirmed and exerted his legitimate authority when it was clearly and practically necessary, and when it was in the best interest of those he was serving. He never used his power for his own advantage. He understood leadership power as always existing to serve the people (2 Cor. 13:10) and not to be served (Matt. 20:28).

the church

The Greek word *ekklesia* (ἐκκλησία) simply means a "gathering" or "assembly." It is not a religious word and is used elsewhere in the New Testament to refer to non-Christian gatherings. Stephen called the people of Israel "the congregation *(ekklesia)* in the wilderness"

(Acts 7:38). In Acts 19:32 and 41 it refers to a mob, and in Acts 19:39 *ekklesia* refers to a convening of citizens to discuss legal matters.[3]

Usually in the New Testament, *ekklesia* refers to the Christian churches.[4] In that context, it always refers to the people of God, and never to buildings. The Early Church had no "church buildings" at all and met usually in private homes (Acts 12:12; 1 Cor. 16:19; Rom. 16:5; Col. 4:15).[5]

> **Relational Dynamic:** The people of God must gather. It is not a legitimate expression of New Testament Christianity for an individual to be an isolated and independent believer with his own private relationship with God. From the beginning, every new church should understand and practice her corporate identity. "Church" means "gathering"! Moreover, there is no single form of that gathering that is mandated anywhere in the New Testament. The church should gather in a wide variety of ways, in different places, at different times and for a multitude of purposes. As long as the people are together with each other, with Jesus as their conscious Head, the gathering will express and nurture life. A healthy church is a gathering church, and in a healthy, gathering church God's people will function!

---

[3] "The term ἐκκλησία was in common usage for several hundred years before the Christian era and was used to refer to an assembly of persons constituted by well-defined membership. In general Greek usage it was normally a socio-political entity based upon citizenship in a city-state." (*Greek-English Lexicon of the New Testament Based on Semantic Domains* by Eugene Nida and Johannes P. Louw)

[4] The word *ekklesia* is used 114 times in the New Testament – 108 of those times it refers to the believers.

[5] The Dura-Europos church in Syria is the earliest identified Christian house church. It was apparently a normal domestic house converted for religious services (it had a baptistry, altar and religious art) sometime between 233 and 256. (Provance, B. S. (2009). In *Pocket Dictionary of Liturgy & Worship* (p. 51). Downers Grove, IL: IVP Academic.) The Aqaba Church in Jordan is considered to be the world's oldest purpose-built Christian church, dated between 293 and 303. (Govier, G. (1998). Archaeology: "Oldest Church" Discovered in Jordan. *Christianity Today, 42*(10), 26.)

> **Instructional Dynamic:** Clearly the believers in Thessalonica understood their identity as the "church" of Jesus Christ. It was not merely that they were a random group of individual believers with personal relationships with God. They were an established and unified spiritual community. Paul had taught them this.

the church of the Thessalonians

There was one church in the city. Paul was able to write a single letter and all the believers would receive it (1 Thess. 5:27). He did not have to write to many churches.

Throughout the New Testament, there was a single church in a town or city (Acts 5:11; 8:1, 3; 14:23; Rom. 1:7; 15:5-7; 16:23; 1 Cor. 1:2; 4:17; 14:23; 2 Cor. 1:1; Eph. 1:1; 4:25; Phil. 1:1; Col. 1:1; 3:15; 4:16; 1 Thess. 1:1; 2 Thess. 1:1; 1 Tim. 1:3; Tit. 1:5; Rev. 1:4, 11) that was made up of many house churches (Rom. 16:5; 1 Cor. 16:19; Col. 4:15; Phm. 2).

> **Relational Dynamic:** From the beginning, the church must be treated as one body. It cannot simply be treated as a religious meeting that many individuals attend, but one body in which all the members need one another, serve one another and share a common purpose. The leaders must intentionally nurture unity.

of the Thessalonians

The city of Thessalonica (now Salonika in Greece and the second-largest city in the nation) was the capital and most important city in Macedonia. The population may have been as high as 200,000 at the time of Paul.

The city was founded in 315 b.c. by Cassander, a general of Alexander the Great. He named the city after his wife Thessalonica, the daughter of Philip of Macedon and the sister of Alexander.

Thessalonica was the seat of Roman administration, had a large harbor and lay on a famous trade route from Rome to the east (the Egnatian Way). Paul and his team probably traveled on this highway. This strategic location would have facilitated the spread of the Gospel from this city to the whole region.

> **Spiritual and Experiential Dynamics:** Paul always sought to be led by the Holy Spirit (e.g., Acts 16:6). At the same time, he thought and acted highly strategically.

There was a significant Jewish population in the city and they had a synagogue (Acts 17:1), but the church was primarily Gentile (they "turned to God from idols," 1:9; also see Acts 17:4).[6]

the church ... in God the Father and the Lord Jesus Christ

This indicates several things about the church of the Thessalonians:

- Oneness – their personal spiritual union with the Father and the Son (1 John 1:1-3).
- Ownership – the church belongs to the Father and the Son.
- Origin – the church was brought into existence from the Father's will and through the work of the Son.
- Otherness – this is a completely different kind of "assembly." It is not a political or social gathering. It is a gathering of the people of God.

---

[6] In the following centuries, the city became a major political and financial Christian center and was called, "The Orthodox City." The "Edict of Thessalonica," issued by three Roman emperors in AD 380, effectively made Nicene Christianity the state religion and church of the Roman Empire. "Nicene Christianity" is a tradition based on the Nicene Creed, which was formulated at the First Council of Nicaea in AD 325 and amended at the First Council of Constantinople in AD 381.

> **Spiritual Dynamic:** The focus of the church must be on God and experiential union with Him – from the beginning and in everything!

> **Instructional Dynamic:** Paul had taught the new believers about the triune nature of God and about our union with Him.

Grace to you and peace

This was Paul's common opening greeting – see his letters to the Romans, Corinthians (both letters), Galatians, Ephesians and Philippians. Through God's grace we have peace with Him and well-being in our lives. This is a beautiful blessing (see also Num. 6:22-27)!

> **Spiritual Dynamic:** Paul's practice was to continually speak blessing to his spiritual sons and daughters.

1:2-3 THANKSGIVING FOR THE THESSALONIANS

2 We give thanks to God always for all of you, constantly mentioning you in our prayers,

We give thanks to God always

What a healthy leader Paul is! Even though he faced such a multitude of sufferings and disappointments, he never lost his continual gratitude to God.

> **Relational Dynamic:** Paul modeled gratitude toward God. This practice nurtured the people's union with Christ as they followed Paul's example of continual gratitude even in the midst of the sufferings they endured.

for all of you

Paul treated them all as one. He embraced them all as God's people. There was no favoritism or special treatment of an elite. All were accepted and loved. All had a seat at the family table.

> **Relational Dynamic:** Paul consciously nurtured a culture of family from the very beginning.

We give thanks to God always for all of you

Paul told them about this. It was not simply a private and confidential practice for him. He wanted them to know he was grateful to God for them. He intentionally told them.

> **Relational Dynamic:** Paul's example built their relationships with one another as they learned to be grateful for each other in spite of differences, disagreements or problems.

constantly mentioning you in our prayers

It seems Paul was praying for their specific needs as well as thanking God for them. These are the two aspects of powerful prayer.

> **Spiritual Dynamic:** Paul's rich and constant prayer is a repeated theme in his letters. Leaders are intercessors! A prayerless leader is a powerless leader. Paul himself prayed for the people; he did not simply pass the prayer requests on to the intercessors. This was the source of the power of his ministry.

our prayers

Paul's whole team was a praying team.

> **Spiritual Dynamic:** Everything Paul did was birthed and sustained in prayer – by him, by his team and by others he solicited to pray for the work.

> **Relational Dynamic:** From the beginning, Paul modeled prayer to the new believers thus helping them toward lives of prayer themselves.

3 remembering before our God and Father your work of faith and labor of love and steadfastness of hope in our Lord Jesus Christ.

remembering

Paul deliberately brought to mind the many good things about the Thessalonians that he could be thankful for. We must be intentional about doing the same, or we will be overwhelmed by the struggles of today and forget the blessings of yesterday.

> **Experiential Dynamic:** By reminding them of their work, their labor and their endurance in all they had suffered, Paul is affirming their lives of obedience to God.

> **Spiritual Dynamic:** Paul's practice of gratefulness was deliberate and thoughtful. Moreover, he told the people specifically why he was grateful for them, thus affirming and encouraging those things.

your work of faith and labor of love and steadfastness of hope

These are the three things Paul was grateful for and the three things he wanted to encourage in their lives. These are the three essential Christian virtues (1 Cor. 13:13). In everything he did, Paul's goal for them was the transformation of their lives!

Paul does not mention church programs here. In fact, he does not mention programs anywhere in his letter. His purpose was life transformation.

> **Relational Dynamic:** The people will do what their leaders affirm. If being on time for meetings is affirmed, then that's what the people will focus on. If the success of programs is what you want, then affirm that and the people will focus on the programs.
>
> But, if faith, love and hope are what you want and what you affirm then that's what the people will focus on. Make sure you affirm the right things! This is how leaders shape culture.
>
> Moreover, since the Thessalonians had been following Jesus for only a short time, their faith, love and hope were not fully mature. Yet Paul affirms them anyway. He didn't withhold his affirmation until they were perfect. He deliberately looked for evidence of life transformation and affirmed those things.

> **Every Member Functions:** In verse 2, Paul mentions "all of you." Then in verse 3, he describes the specific fruit of their lives. Every member was functioning! Every member was connected with God, serving each other, building one another, reaching out. They were not passive spectators at a religious performance on Sunday. They were all active participants in the broad life of the church.

your work of faith

Their work was the result of their faith. They did not merely have an intellectual belief but a real faith in God that resulted in works

(Jam. 2:14-26). Paul does not affirm their mental assent of the truth of the Gospel, but their work of repentance and obedience in response to it.

> **Instructional Dynamic:** Paul had taught them about salvation by faith and that faith will result in works of faith.

labor of love

The Greek word for "labor" means to work hard. It can be used in contexts of difficult or even agonizing labor. The work of loving and serving one another can be quite challenging at times!

> **Instructional Dynamic:** Paul had taught them to love one another in deed (1 John 3:16-18).

steadfastness of hope

"Steadfastness" means endurance, perseverance, constancy in the face of difficulty. The Thessalonians experienced considerable opposition for the sake of the Gospel (Acts 17:5-6) but they did not give up because their hope was set on eternal glory! They endured the troubles without self-pity or discouragement.

> **The Four Facets:** Faith toward God results in holiness, righteousness, worship and so forth. Love toward the brethren results in care, kindness, forgiveness, servanthood and so forth. Hope toward the future results in endurance, in building the next generation, and in reaching out to the lost with the message of eternal hope. Paul highly valued all three and so he taught them, looked for them, remembered them and affirmed them. His purpose was not to establish a religious organization with highly functioning programs. His goal was to build a people of faith, love and hope! His goal was life transformation.
>
> These are the key indicators of the health of a church – faith, love and hope – not the Sunday morning attendance or the amount of money in the church's bank account.

in our Lord Jesus Christ

This means "in union with Christ." Throughout all his letters, Paul continually points every believer to union with Christ. This is not merely a legal standing before God, but an inward experience of fellowship with Jesus by His Spirit.

> **Instructional Dynamic:** Paul had taught the believer's union with Christ to these new Christians. It is a foundational teaching.

1:4-10 THE ESTABLISHING OF THE THESSALONIAN CHURCH

4 For we know, brothers loved by God, that He has chosen you,

For we know

Their faith, love and hope are the practical and unmistakable proofs that God has chosen them to be His.

brothers

The Greek word (*adelphoi*) literally means "brothers," but it can also be used to indicate "brothers and sisters."[7] Here, Paul is clearly referring to all the believers, the family of God.

loved by God

Before the creation of the world God loved His people and chose them to be His (Eph. 1:4). This is why we can endure the hardships now – the eternal love of God is upon us and His love will never fail!

---

7 Arndt, W., Danker, F. W., Bauer, W., & Gingrich, F. W. (2000). *A Greek-English Lexicon of the New Testament and Other Early Christian Literature* (3rd ed., p. 18). Chicago: University of Chicago Press.

5 because our Gospel came to you not only in Word, but also in power and in the Holy Spirit and with full conviction. You know what kind of men we proved to be among you for your sake.

because

The way the Gospel came to them is further proof that God has loved them and called them to know Him.

not only in Word

They heard the Word of Truth in the Gospel. The Word of God has the power to transform lives, but it must be the Word of God – not human theories or traditions, not philosophical speculations, not political or social opinions, not pleasant messages on how to be successful in life. Churches are planted through the teaching of the Word of God!

not only … but also …

In the structure of the underlying Greek text, the "but also …" is emphasized.[8]

This is not in any way a denigration of the power of the Word of God. It is simply an affirmation that the teaching of the Word must be accompanied by the other three Dynamics.[9]

---

8   Source: *The Lexham Discourse Greek New Testament*.
9   The other three Dynamics of Transformation are Spiritual, Relational and Experiential.

> **Instructional Dynamic:** This is a profound statement of the power of the Word of God to save the lost and to establish churches. However, it is "not only" the Word that is necessary. All four Dynamics are vital and all four were present when Paul planted the Thessalonian church. Paul was deliberate about using all four.

in power and in the Holy Spirit and with full conviction

This includes the anointing of the Holy Spirit upon the teaching of the Word, the conviction of the Holy Spirit upon the hearts of the hearers, and, quite likely, signs and wonders accompanying the Word. The Holy Spirit was personally present and extensively active in the planting of this church. Church planting is His work and we have the privilege of being co-laborers with Him (1 Cor. 3:6-9).

> **Spiritual Dynamic:** The church was planted through a powerful moving of the Holy Spirit. In everything we must depend on Him and let Him have His way.

You know what kind of men we proved to be among you for your sake

Paul not only taught the Word of God – he also lived it before the people he served.

for your sake

Paul did everything for the sake of the people. He was always conscious of what was in their best interests, and not his own. This is the essence of servant leadership (Matt. 20:26-28; Phil. 2:4, 20-21).

> **Relational Dynamic:** The Truth of the Word of God and the power of the Holy Spirit must be matched by the sincerity and integrity of the lives of those who proclaim it.

6 And you became imitators of us and of the Lord, for you received the Word in much affliction, with the joy of the Holy Spirit,

you became imitators of us and of the Lord, for you received the Word

This is the final evidence that God loved them and chose them: the Thessalonians believed the Word, repented and obeyed the Word. As a result, they were persecuted.

> **Experiential Dynamic:** Without having obeyed the Word, the Thessalonians would not have been saved and the church would not have been planted. It is when we obey God that we are changed (Jam. 2:14-26). This means that our teaching must always be practical, not only theoretical; if there is no clear path of obedience then what is the value of teaching something? The true Gospel is always practical and always requires action.

imitators of us and of the Lord

They imitated their spiritual parents (Paul and his team) and the Lord.

> **Relational Dynamic:** They not only obeyed Paul's specific teaching, they also imitated his way of life. In addition, they were persecuted just as Paul and Jesus before him were persecuted.

in much affliction

Much persecution accompanied Paul's initial ministry in Thessalonica (Acts 17:5-9). We can assume that it continued after his departure since the Jews from Thessalonica were so zealous in opposing him that they followed him to Berea to stir up trouble for him there (Acts 17:13). Presumably, they continued to severely persecute the new church in Thessalonica. Moreover, since Thessalonica was heavily pagan and idolatrous, they would also have been persecuted by the Gentiles!

> **Experiential Dynamic:** True leaders will not interpret trouble and suffering as evidence of God's displeasure or as reasons for giving up. If we follow Jesus we will experience the same rejection that He experienced (Matt. 10:25). Moreover, it is through union with Christ in His sufferings and death that we will experience deeper union with Him in His life (2 Cor. 12:9).

with the joy of the Holy Spirit

This refers to the joy given by the Holy Spirit. God does not leave us to experience the persecution in our own strength. As we look to Him, the presence of the Holy Spirit brings us special comfort in the midst of the sufferings (2 Cor. 1:3-7).

In Christ, we have so much reason for joy: we rejoice that we are saved, that we are blessed, that we have eternal hope, that we know

God, that we are in Christ, and that we are counted worthy to suffer for Him.

Our circumstances do not dictate whether we have joy or not – our union with Christ does!

> **Spiritual Dynamic:** The church must continually look to the Holy Spirit, depending on Him and receiving His comfort and joy. The work of the Holy Spirit must never simply be a theory to us – He is real and active in our midst. Inwardly, we must look at Him and connect with Him (2 Cor. 3:18).

7 so that you became an example to all the believers in Macedonia and in Achaia.

you became an example to all the believers

The Thessalonians were a healthy church! Of course, they were not perfect; later in this letter and in 2 Thessalonians, Paul addresses areas of concern. But they were healthy, and they were a model for other churches – including our churches today – to follow.

As they followed Paul's example, they themselves became an example to the churches that were planted after them. They were only the second church in the region to be established, after the Philippian church.

to all the believers

Every member was functioning in the Thessalonian church (1 Thess. 1:2-3). Paul's hope was that every member of the other churches would follow their example.

in Macedonia and in Achaia

The Thessalonians influenced many others in a large geographical region. The map below shows the extent of their influence – all the way to Achaia!

Wider Church: The Thessalonians clearly had ongoing and very positive relationships with the wider Body of Christ in their region (1 Thess. 4:9-10). Other churches knew them, followed their example and spoke highly of them (1 Thess. 1:9). They were not competing with each other. They were speaking well of one another.

8 For not only has the Word of the Lord sounded forth from you in Macedonia and Achaia, but your faith in God has gone forth everywhere, so that we need not say anything.

the Word of the Lord sounded forth from you in Macedonia and Achaia

This healthy church had tremendous ministry impact – across two provinces! This was not because they initiated formal "outreach programs" but powerful impact across their entire region occurred as the natural result of being a healthy church.

> **Every Member Reaches Out:** Their evangelistic impact was through the personal lives and testimonies of these transformed believers as their neighbors heard about their faith in God. Every member functioned – every member reached out!

> **The Four Dynamics of Transformation:** In the entire New Testament, Paul's words in 1 Thessalonians 1:5-8 are perhaps the clearest and most comprehensive expressions of his use and the power of the Four Dynamics. Through the Four Dynamics, the Thessalonians became a healthy church and one that had tremendous ministry impact in a large geographical region!

your faith in God has gone forth everywhere

Not only have the Thessalonians shared the Gospel extensively but the report of their own transformation has also been widely heard.

> **Instructional Dynamic:** Paul had taught them the need to share their faith. He had also taught them enough so that they were able to do so.

so that we need not say anything

Everyone has already heard about the faith of the Thessalonians so Paul didn't need to speak about it. Of course, he would have anyway!

All of this demonstrates the powerful life transformation that has occurred in the church of the Thessalonians.

9 For they themselves report concerning us the kind of reception we had among you, and how you turned to God from idols to serve the living and true God,

they themselves report

Other believers in Macedonia and Achaia were reporting to Paul about the lives and fruit of the church in Thessalonica. The Thessalonians were well known – for the fruit of their lives, for their bold and effective witness in the face of opposition, and for their impact on other churches.

Paul would often boast to others about the various churches he served (e.g., 2 Cor. 9:2). This time people were boasting to him about the Thessalonians!

> **Relational Dynamic:** Paul genuinely loved the churches he established. He was proud of them and he spoke affectionately to them and about them to others. What a life-building thing this is when the leader boasts about his people, instead of criticizing them and finding fault!

you turned to God from idols to serve the living and true God

Most of the Thessalonian believers were Gentiles. Thessalonica was full of idolatry; they worshiped many pagan gods (Greek, Roman and Egyptian) along with accompanying immoral behavior. Now, by the power of the Holy Spirit and through the truth of God's Word, these Gentiles have turned to serve the living and true God!

There were three groups of people who came to Christ in Thessalonica: a few Jews and many devout Gentiles (Acts 17:4), and also pagan Gentiles (1 Thess. 1:9).

> **Instructional Dynamic:** Paul had taught against idols immediately. This was his usual practice (Acts 19:26). He did not leave this until later.

the living and true God

In contrast to the dead and false idols they used to serve.

> **Experiential Dynamic:** The kind of reception Paul speaks of is not that they merely mentally agreed with the Word he taught them. It was that they obeyed the Word. They turned away from their idols and began to serve the true God. This is what people observed about them and reported so positively.

> **Instructional Dynamic:** Paul had taught against idolatry and showed them the empty nature of what they had been serving.

10 and to wait for His Son from heaven, whom He raised from the dead, Jesus who delivers us from the wrath to come.

to wait for His Son from heaven

One of Paul's main reasons for writing to the Thessalonians was to encourage them to endure through their sufferings. Our hope of Jesus' imminent return gives us the greatest encouragement possible.

Every chapter in this letter ends with a reference to Jesus' return (1 Thess. 1:10; 2:19; 3:13; 4:13-18, 5:23). Of course, Paul did not write in chapters[10] but this does show how prominent a theme Jesus' return is in the letter.

to wait

This is not a passive waiting, but an active and continuous attitude of expectancy. Paul expects Jesus to return soon (1 Thess. 4:15). We long for His return and we must always be ready (Matt. 25:1-13). Because Jesus is returning soon, how will we live, what will we do? The Thessalonians' aggressive evangelism, for example, is an appropriate action.

> **Experiential Dynamic:** The doctrine of Jesus' return should directly motivate all believers to reach out to other people with the Gospel.

---

[10] Chapter divisions were added to the New Testament much later – in 1227. The modern verse divisions in the New Testament were added in 1551.

whom He raised from the dead

Jesus' resurrection was the proof of His deity (Rom. 1:4; 1 Cor. 15:14-19) and the guarantee that God will one day also raise us up from the dead (Phil. 3:20-21).

> **Instructional Dynamic:** Paul had taught the new believers about Jesus' death, resurrection and soon return.

who delivers us

God has delivered us, is delivering us, and will deliver us. Salvation will be finally complete after the resurrection (Rom. 8:23; Eph. 1:14).

the wrath to come

This wrath includes the Great Tribulation (Rev. 7:14), but is not limited to that. We are delivered from all of God's eternal judgment through Jesus' death.

All those who oppose God, including those who now persecute the Thessalonians (1 Thess. 2:16), will be destroyed by God's wrath (2 Thess. 1:6-9).

> **Instructional Dynamic:** Paul had taught the new believers about God's eternal judgment of sinners.

Chapter 2

2:1-12 PAUL'S MINISTRY IN THESSALONICA

1 For you yourselves know, brothers, that our coming to you was not in vain.

For you yourselves know

Not only do others report such good things about you (1 Thess. 1:9), but you know it to be true yourselves.

our coming to you was not in vain

Far from being "in vain" (the Greek word means "empty"), Paul's coming was full of power (1 Thess. 1:5) and resulted in great impact (1 Thess. 1:6-10).

2 But though we had already suffered and been shamefully treated at Philippi, as you know, we had boldness in our God to declare to you the Gospel of God in the midst of much conflict.

we had already suffered and been shamefully treated at Philippi

Just before they came to Thessalonica, Paul and his team planted a church at Philippi, where they were fiercely persecuted (Acts 16:11-40). Paul and Silas had been attacked, arrested, slandered, stripped of their clothes, publicly beaten, imprisoned, and put in stocks in Philippi.

While in prison, they had responded with prayer and singing hymns to God and then God supernaturally delivered them. However, Paul's focus here is on the persecution, since that is immediately relevant to the Thessalonians.

> **Instructional Dynamic:** When teaching the Word we should focus on what is immediately relevant to those we serve. Moreover, we should only use our own examples when they benefit our hearers – rather than just talking about ourselves because we enjoy it or want to show off.

as you know

It was quite likely that Paul had told the Thessalonians about his experiences of rejection and persecution in Philippi, and perhaps in other cities also.

> **Relational Dynamic:** Leaders should share about their own sufferings with the people they serve (e.g., 2 Cor. 1:8). In this way, the people of God will face the reality of what it means to be a follower of Jesus and will count the cost themselves.

> **Instructional Dynamic:** Paul taught about sufferings to new believers. He did not consider it a more advanced truth to be only dealt with later. The fact is that new believers will often *immediately* face persecution – as well as sufferings of every kind – so they need to understand those sufferings in the light of the Gospel.

we had boldness in our God

The rejection and persecution they experienced at Philippi would have been enough to deter many men, but Paul and his team found their courage and boldness in their union with Christ.

> **Spiritual Dynamic:** Paul did not find strength in his own human tenacity, but in his life in God. Those who plant and lead churches must do so out of their inner spiritual relationship with God. Then they will impart life to others.

to declare to you the Gospel of God in the midst of much conflict

Just as Paul's team had been persecuted in Philippi, now they also had "much conflict" in Thessalonica.

> **Experiential Dynamic:** When the true Gospel is presented and takes root, we should expect it to be opposed. Healthy churches are born in the fire of suffering. This doesn't mean we should seek suffering, but we should not be surprised when it happens and we should embrace the opportunity that it gives us to find God more deeply (1 Pet. 4:12-19). Pressure and suffering will be the inevitable lot of both the church planter and the planted church.

much conflict

The Greek word for "conflict" means an intense struggle against strong opposition. This is the nature of the Christian life and true ministry! The Thessalonian church was born in the fire.

Moreover, the church planter must work very hard ("struggle"). Success will not come easily. We're in a constant battle. We must fight!

3 For our appeal does not spring from error or impurity or any attempt to deceive,

For

This is the grounds for Paul's boldness in the face of fierce opposition: the sincerity and integrity of his ministry and his deep conviction in God's calling.

our appeal

As Paul shared the Gospel, he urgently exhorted the people to receive it, and to repent and obey the truth.

> **Experiential Dynamic:** Paul did not share truth with people for the purpose of them agreeing with it. He presented the Gospel and then expected and urged them to obey it. Our teaching – on every subject – must always result in practical steps of action.

error

Paul and his team were not deceived themselves. They knew the truth.

> **Instructional Dynamic:** Paul was in no doubt about what he taught to others. We should teach only what we know well. Moreover, we should not teach peripheral issues to new believers. The new church must be founded on solid, essential teaching on major issues – not on marginal issues or human traditions.

impurity

The Greek word means moral corruption. It is often used of sexual sins but is not limited to that. Some of the impure motives that could drive church planters are: financial greed, ambition, power, pride, fame and popularity.

any attempt to deceive

Paul was not deceived and he did not deceive others. His motive was pure. As a true servant leader, his only motive was the good of the people.

> **Relational Dynamic:** A healthy church planter will build healthy churches. The leader's own life will ultimately be reflected in those he leads. Therefore, the leader must have integrity.

The fire of persecution also tests the leader's life and ministry. If he does this work for some self-centered motive, he won't be able to stand when trouble comes but will run, hide and protect himself (John 10:12). But the true leader with sincere motives before God will stand. Thus, personal integrity is far more the necessary foundation of a leader's ministry than intellectual or academic achievement.

4 but just as we have been approved by God to be entrusted with the Gospel, so we speak, not to please man, but to please God who tests our hearts.

approved by God to be entrusted with the Gospel

Because of his sincerity and purity, God approved Paul and gave him the assignment of preaching the Gospel.

so we speak

As God was the center of Paul's preparation and the focus of his motives, so He was the only one Paul sought to please with his teaching.

not to please man, but to please God

True spiritual ministry will certainly be good for men when they receive it, but the ultimate motive of the leader is always to serve God.

Vision is central to leadership. But the vision itself must be "legitimate." A "legitimate vision" means two things. First, the vision must genuinely be the will of God – consistent with the spiritual nature of healthy leadership. Apart from union with Christ, we can accomplish nothing of any value (John 15:4-5). A legitimate vision comes from God. Then it becomes the leader's own vision – something he can share passionately with others, calling them to sacrifice and endurance in its pursuit. Without the divine initiation, man's vision is mere human ambition.

Second, a legitimate vision will genuinely reflect what is good for the people, and not only what is good for the leader – consistent with the servant nature of healthy leadership (Mark 10:45).

God who tests our hearts

The verb "tests" is in the present tense, indicating it was continuous. God continually tested Paul's thoughts and motives. God did not do this for His own benefit – He fully knows everything in our hearts and lives. He did it for Paul's benefit so that he would, in the end, succeed, and for the benefit of those Paul served so they would be saved.

> **Spiritual Dynamic:** We see Paul's constant reflection before God here. He continually brought his heart, motives and vision before God to be tested and purified. In addition, when God brought deep things in Paul's heart to the surface and exposed them, he responded with repentance and commitment.
>
> This indicates the leader's need for regular reflection and personal evaluation. We see this in Jesus' ministry. He continually came apart to spend time with His Father. If Jesus did that so frequently,[11] how much more must we?

---

11   The Gospel of Luke gives us a close look at how often Jesus came apart for special time with His Father (Luke 3:21-22; 4:1-13; 4:42-44; 5:15-16; 6:12; 9:18, 28-29; 11:1-4; 22:31-32, 22:39-46; 23:34, 46). Jesus did this all the time!

5 For we never came with words of flattery, as you know, nor with a pretext for greed – God is witness.

For

This is the grounds for his previous statements (1 Thess. 2:3-4).

never

Paul was able to say this. May we also be able to say this of our own ministries!

words of flattery

Paul did frequently compliment people. Flattery, however, is manipulative and exploits others for one's own purposes. Paul never flattered people; he told them the truth.

as you know

Paul's personal integrity and purity of ministry was obvious to those he served. They knew him. This meant they had the opportunity to know him; they did not only see him on Sunday morning when he stood on a platform and publicly taught. He lived with them.

> **Relational Dynamic:** Jesus called His disciples to "be with Him" (Mark 3:14). This is how leaders and disciples are built; not through "celebrity" ministry from a platform, but in the daily context of normal life. This involves a high level of transparency from the leader and a deep commitment to doing the true work of spiritual ministry.

nor with a pretext for greed

Paul never pretended to be something he wasn't for the sake of personal gain.

God is witness

While the Thessalonians could testify to his purity of conduct ("as you know"), God could testify to his purity of motive.

6 Nor did we seek glory from people, whether from you or from others, though we could have made demands as apostles of Christ.

glory

The Greek word literally means "glory"; it is the word used in the New Testament for the glory of God. Here it has the sense of honor, praise, applause or fame. Paul certainly deserved and would have received some honor, and he taught the people to honor their leaders (1 Thess. 5:12), but he never sought honor.

At that time, itinerant philosophers and orators were common in the Roman Empire. They traveled around and entertained the people, seeking a personal following for money and fame. In contrast, Paul and his team delighted in giving freely to those they served (1 Thess. 2:9; 2 Cor. 2:17).

Today, we live in a celebrity-saturated culture – so many seek money and fame. Like Paul, the true Christian leader will have nothing to do with this, but will give freely.

It's possible that Paul's persecutors were accusing him of these various false motives, and he is appealing to the Thessalonians' own experience of his life and ministry before them to defend himself.

whether from you or from others

Paul was not trying to impress the Thessalonians or anyone else, including his detractors, but only God.

we could have made demands as apostles of Christ

As apostles, Paul, Silas and Timothy could have required honor and money from the people, but they did not. The Greek here means to be weighty or authoritative. They refused to "throw their weight around." This is the character and practice of the true apostle (2 Cor. 1:24).

> **Relational Dynamic:** Everything that a leader does shapes the culture of the church. Paul is careful to live and serve selflessly; thus, he builds a healthy church. Paul did this consciously and deliberately to set an example (2 Thess. 3:9). A self-giving leader builds a self-giving church. A competitive and self-seeking leader builds a competitive and self-seeking church.

apostles of Christ

1 Thessalonians is possibly the first book written by Paul[12]; if so, then this is the very first use of the word "apostle" in his writings – in the context of not using his apostolic authority! The true apostle has authority but chooses not to use it unless absolutely necessary (e.g., 2 Cor. 13:10). Instead he chooses servanthood, gentleness and self-giving love.

---

12 Some scholars believe that First and Second Thessalonians were the first books written by Paul. Others believe that Galatians was.

Fivefold Ministry: Paul's understanding of the "Fivefold Ministry" is very different from the current popular understanding. To Paul, having one of the five ministry offices of Ephesians 4:11 did not mean entitlement, power or status. It meant responsibility to do a particular kind of work in a particular way.

Those who truly have one of these five offices will do the same. Instead of seeking prominence and acclaim, they will do the hard work of serving God's people with a self-giving spirit of humility and sacrifice, not caring about the praise of men.

Instructional Dynamic: Throughout this letter, and during his time with them, Paul establishes the nature of spiritual authority – true servant leadership.

7 But we were gentle among you, like a nursing mother taking care of her own children.

But we were gentle among you

Paul and his team could have been self-asserting and demanding, but instead they were gentle. The Greek word for "gentle" literally means infant or child. This is a beautiful image of humility, innocence, purity and gentleness.

among you

Paul was not just passively "with" them. Neither did he only see them once a week for a Sunday morning meeting. He lived among them, closely and deeply interacting with them. The Greek word could be translated "in the middle."

> **Relational Dynamic:** Paul lived in the middle of those he served. He knew them. They knew him. This is how healthy churches are built. Church life is a daily sharing of life; the leaders cannot be removed from this. This was how Jesus built His disciples – He also lived "in the middle" of them. "For who is the greater, one who reclines at table or one who serves? Is it not the one who reclines at table? But I am among you as the One who serves." (Luke 22:27)

like a nursing mother taking care of her own children

Paul describes very close attention and deep care. Is there any more powerful way to express that than this image?

her own children

A mother will certainly be loving toward the children of others. But toward her own children, there is no simpler or purer love (Gal. 4:19).

In the previous verses, Paul disassociates himself from motives of greed and selfishness. Here he presents an extraordinary motive of pure self-giving.

8 So, being affectionately desirous of you, we were ready to share with you not only the Gospel of God but also our own selves, because you had become very dear to us.

affectionately desirous ... you had become very dear to us

Paul's relationship with the Thessalonians was not a professional one. He was genuinely affectionate toward them (Phil. 1:8).

we were ready to share with you not only the
Gospel of God but also our own selves

A nursing mother will give anything for her own children – including her own life – without hesitation. This is the depth of Paul's love (John 15:13). He not only taught them, he shared his life with them.

> **Relational Dynamic:** Paul's specific purpose for the new church was that the Thessalonians would love and serve one another. Therefore, he first loved them. However, it was not just a forced attempt at love because he knew he had to love them. His love for the people was genuine and deep.
>
> The leader must have a real love for the people he serves. Often leaders treat the people as "necessary evils." They try to love them because they know they should, but in their hearts they're angry and frustrated with the people. Such leaders must get right with God! Only truly loving leaders will build a truly loving church.

9 For you remember, brothers, our labor and toil: we worked night and day, that we might not be a burden to any of you, while we proclaimed to you the Gospel of God.

For

This is the proof of Paul's self-giving love for the Thessalonians: that he worked night and day to not be a burden to them, while sharing his life and teaching with them.

Paul was a true servant leader – he put the good of the people before himself. He was very careful about not being a financial burden to them lest that become a stumbling block to anyone (2 Cor. 11:9).

Elsewhere, Paul taught the appropriateness of leaders receiving financial support from the people they served (e.g., 1 Cor. 9; 1 Tim. 5:17-18) but if there ever was any doubt about how this would be taken, he declined that right and worked as a tentmaker to support himself.

We know that Paul received two financial gifts from the Philippians while in Thessalonica (Phil. 4:16); presumably that was not enough to fully support Paul and his team.

you remember

The Thessalonians knew well how Paul had lived. Therefore, they trusted his motives and believed his teaching. In addition, they themselves learned how to live as children of God and serve one another.

labor and toil

The first word refers to the work itself and the second refers to the hardship of that work. Paul embraced this difficult lifestyle because of his love for the Thessalonians.

Relational Dynamic: Paul's purpose for the Thessalonians was that they would work hard and take care of each other. Therefore, he deliberately modeled this himself (Acts 20:33-35). Later he taught this (2 Thess. 3:6-15). Like Jesus, Paul did and then taught (Acts 1:1).

10 You are witnesses, and God also, how holy and righteous and blameless was our conduct toward you believers.

You are witnesses, and God also

The Thessalonians knew Paul's life and God knew his heart.

holy and righteous and blameless

The three words are similar in meaning; together they create a strong affirmation of Paul's integrity.

This whole passage (1 Thess. 2:3-10) stands as an extraordinary rebuke of the current popular approach to apostleship. Today's "apostle" is often a celebrity who demands to be the center of attention and to be given titles, deference and money. He lives entirely removed from the people except when he deigns to appear once in a while to give a boasting and self-promoting religious performance from a stage. Such "apostles" were around in his time also, and Paul harshly condemned them both by his example and his teaching (2 Cor. 11).

11 For you know how, like a father with his children,

For

This is why the Thessalonians are witnesses to Paul's integrity (1 Thess. 2:10).

you know

This is the fifth time up to this point that Paul wrote "you know." In the whole letter he refers to the Thessalonians' personal knowledge of his life and teaching no less than ten times (1 Thess. 1:5; 2:1, 2, 5, 9, 10, 11; 3:3, 4; 4:2)! Once again, we see Paul's life "in the middle" of the Thessalonians. He was not some distant religious professional. They knew him well. This is the ministry of a true apostle: no dramatic performance from a stage by an entitled celebrity, just the intense, hard work of life together with the people of God.

like a father with his children

In verse 7, Paul compared his care for the people with the self-giving love of a nursing mother. Now he compares his instruction of the people with a responsible father who is entirely committed to the well-being and success of his children. In the Old Testament, God also spoke of Himself both as a mother (Is. 66:13) and as a father (Ps. 103:13) toward Israel. Paul nurtured the Thessalonians like a mother and instructed them like a father.

Paul treated the Thessalonians as a father treats "his own children" (Greek). Out of his deep and affectionate concern for them, he exhorted, encouraged and charged them (1 Thess. 2:12).

> **Relational Dynamic:** Paul repeatedly uses family metaphors in this chapter. To him, the "church" was not a building or a formal Sunday morning meeting. It was the lives of the saints joined together in the family of God.

12 we exhorted each one of you and encouraged you and charged you to walk in a manner worthy of God, who calls you into His own Kingdom and glory.

Exhorted ... encouraged ... charged

Three similar but distinct kinds of verbal instruction: exhortation, encouragement and insisting on obedience ("charging"). You *should* do this! You *can* do this! You *must* do this!

> **Experiential Dynamic:** Paul insisted on their obedience! He was not content that they merely understood and believed his teaching.

each one of you ... to walk in a manner worthy of God

Paul's purpose for them was life transformation, not merely church attendance or participation in church programs. This is the highest calling possible – to live a life worthy of God! And this was Paul's purpose for *each one* of them (Col. 1:28).

Instructional Dynamic: Paul's instruction to the Thessalonians was rich and diverse. He did not give them lectures on abstract theories. He exhorted, encouraged and charged them in the context of their lives. His teaching was practical and always focused on life transformation (living a life "worthy of God") – never just on intellectual agreement.

Every Member Functions: Paul's hope was for every one of the Thessalonians to live in a manner worthy of the God who called them. He had no interest in them passively watching him doing the work. They were all participants!

Fivefold Ministry: Clearly the role of the leaders is to equip all of God's people that they will do the work of the ministry (Eph. 4:12). Through the Presence and power of the Holy Spirit, his own example and loving care, the expectation for obedience to the Word, and the practical teaching of the Word of God (Four Dynamics of Transformation), Paul nurtured a healthy culture in the Thessalonian church in which every member functioned.

God, who calls you into His own Kingdom and glory

This is the ultimate destiny of all disciples: the eternal Kingdom and glory of God (John 17:24; 2 Cor. 4:17; Col. 3:4)!

Verses 10-12 give a summary of Paul's work in Thessalonica. He lived among them and taught them by his own example and by his own practical teaching, always urging obedience and focusing on life transformation for every member of the church.

2:13-16 THE THESSALONIANS' RECEPTION OF THE GOSPEL

13 And we also thank God constantly for this, that when you received the Word of God, which you heard from us, you accepted it not as the word of men but as what it really is, the Word of God, which is at work in you believers.

Having just described how the Word of God was delivered to them, Paul now speaks about how they received it.

we also thank God constantly

Paul mentions his constant gratitude to God again (1 Thess. 1:2-3) as he thinks about how the Thessalonians received the Word.

which you heard from us

Before the Gospels were written, the Word of God was passed along orally. This had to be done in person since there were no phones, internet or television. Yet the Word of God spread rapidly and powerfully (Acts 17:6)!

you received ... you accepted ...

Paul uses two different Greek verbs. The first indicates an objective receiving; in this case they listened to the Word. The second indicates a subjective, internal response of approval to what they heard. They accepted it as God's Word and not man's, and they believed it and acted on it. As a result, it changed their lives.

what it really is, the Word of God

Paul had no doubt that what he taught was the true Word of God (Gal. 1:11-12).

> **Instructional Dynamic:** Paul taught what he knew for certain was the Word of God – rather than peripheral or unclear doctrines. A healthy church is built on core truths! Therefore, the church planter must teach the Word (and not the ideas or traditions of man) and he must teach the core Word (and not peripheral or unclear doctrines). The foundation of the new church must be sound.

which is at work in you believers

Unlike the word of man, the Word of God is powerful. When the Word is taught – rather than human logic or traditions – it works deeply and quickly. After only a few months of Paul's teachings, the Thessalonians were able to thrive!

14 For you, brothers, became imitators of the churches of God in Christ Jesus that are in Judea. For you suffered the same things from your own countrymen as they did from the Jews,

you, brothers, became imitators of the churches of God

They obeyed the Word and consequently were persecuted for their faith. This is how Paul knew they had received it. They were not persecuted for agreeing with doctrinal theories about Christ – they were persecuted for the life transformation they experienced in their obedience to His Word.

imitators

They were not consciously imitating them. Paul means that the same persecution that had happened to the Judean churches was now happening to them.

Throughout the New Testament, persecution is a major indicator of true faith – in the Gospels, in Acts, in the Epistles, and in Revelation!

the churches of God in Christ Jesus that are in Judea

Paul always connected every local church with the wider Body of Christ.

> **Instructional Dynamic:** From the beginning, Paul taught the Thessalonians that they were a part of the wider church.

> **Relational Dynamic:** Most, if not all, of the Thessalonians had not personally met the Judean churches. They heard about them from Paul. Paul not only used his own example but also the examples of others to build life.

your own countrymen

In Thessalonica, the Jews stirred up the Gentiles to persecute them (Acts 17:5).

15 who killed both the Lord Jesus and the prophets, and drove us out, and displease God and oppose all mankind

who killed ... the Lord Jesus

It was the Romans who actually killed Jesus, but the Jewish leaders instigated it (Acts 3:13-15).

> **Instructional Dynamic:** Paul had taught them about the life and death of the Lord Jesus.

the prophets

The Old Testament prophets (Luke 13:34).

drove us out

Refers to Paul and his team (Acts 17:10, 14).

displease God

This was not their conscious attempt. They thought they were pleasing Him – as Paul did when he persecuted the church (Acts 22:3-4). From God's side, however, He was very displeased.

oppose all mankind

They hindered the work of the Gospel going to the Gentiles (see next verse).

16 by hindering us from speaking to the Gentiles that they might be saved – so as always to fill up the measure of their sins. But wrath has come upon them at last!

by hindering us from speaking to the Gentiles

Paul wrote this letter to the Thessalonians when he was in Corinth. During that time, he was severely persecuted by the Jews (Acts 18:5-12), something that was common for him and for the churches he planted.

always

The Jews persecuted the servants of God in the Old Testament, then the Lord Jesus, and now Paul and the apostles.

fill up the measure of their sins

This is a metaphor of filling up a cup (see Gen. 15:16; Dan. 8:23; Matt. 23:32[13]). The idea is that when the cup is full then God will judge them. God alone knows when the cup will be full; until then He doesn't pour out His final judgment. By persecuting the believers, the Jews are hastening their judgment.

wrath has come

This is literally, "the wrath" – the coming judgment of God. It is still in the future, but it's so near and so certain in Paul's mind that he says it has already come.

These words are not shared in bitterness by Paul; in his heart he deeply loved the Jews (Rom. 9:1-5; 10:1-2). Jesus also dearly loved the Jews, while declaring the reality of God's just punishment upon them (Matt. 23:37-39; Luke 19:41-44).

---

13   This metaphor is also found in the Apocrypha (2 Macc. 6:14).

at last

God's wrath has reached the point where it will soon pass into judgment.

2:17-20 PAUL'S LONGING FOR THE THESSALONIANS

17 But since we were torn away from you, brothers, for a short time, in person not in heart, we endeavored the more eagerly and with great desire to see you face to face,

But

In verses 1-16, Paul referred to this time with the Thessalonians. Now he shifts his focus to the time since they left the city.

we were torn away from you

The Greek means "to make an orphan of." This indicates the intense personal relationship between Paul and the Thessalonians. The separation was like that between parents and children. Once more, Paul uses family language to describe his relationship with the Thessalonians (1 Thess. 2:7-8, 11).

Significantly, the abrupt departure of Paul (Acts 17:10) did not destroy the church. By the time he left, the church had been deeply and soundly established.

for a short time

It was several months, but due to his love for the Thessalonians, it must have seemed like a very long time to Paul.

in person not in heart

They were separated physically, but Paul's thoughts and affection were still with them. He deeply loved and cared for them.

There is a contrast here between the short time and short distance ("in person not in heart") of their separation with the intensity of Paul's longing to be reunited with them.

18 because we wanted to come to you – I, Paul, again and again – but Satan hindered us.

I, Paul, again and again

The intensity of Paul's desire to return. This could have been when he was in Berea, Athens or Corinth.

but Satan hindered us

We don't know exactly what Paul meant by this. Perhaps this refers to the Jews constantly stirring up trouble in Thessalonica that prevented him from returning. In any case, this is the constant battle of the leader; everything does not always work out – even for Paul!

> **Experiential Dynamic:** Healthy leaders are built in the fire. Healthy churches are also built in the fire.

Satan

The Greek word for Satan was borrowed from Aramaic and originally meant, "one lying in ambush for."[14]

---

14   There was a papyrus example from the third century B.C. in which the verb was used to mean "to cut in a road, to make a road impassable."

When referring to the devil, this became a proper name: "the adversary" or "the accuser." Paul directly attributed the work of his human opposition to the instigation of the devil. At other times in his ministry, God prevented him from doing something (Acts 16:6-7).

hindered

The Greek for "hindered" is literally, "to cut a trench between one's self and an advancing foe, to prevent his progress." It means to make progress slow or difficult.[15]

19 For what is our hope or joy or crown of boasting before our Lord Jesus at His coming? Is it not you?

our hope

Paul is confident that the Thessalonians will do well, endure, and come to maturity, and that he will be able to present them before God in victory on the Last Day. "Hope" is a somewhat weak word in English, but in Paul's vocabulary it expresses his absolute confidence in the certainty of the future. Jesus has guaranteed our eternal life by His death and resurrection!

joy

Standing together with them before Jesus at His coming will bring great rejoicing to Paul.

---

15 On a side note, when people respond in a passive-aggressive way to hinder a leader, they are literally performing the work of the devil.

what is our ... crown of boasting ... Is it not you?

To Paul, a "crown" is not a symbol of royalty but the (usually laurel) wreath given to the winner in the athletic games. It is the symbol of victory, of achievement. Paul is picturing himself as standing in the Lord's Presence at His return, wearing the victor's wreath and the "wreath" is the Thessalonian believers themselves.

Paul will boast about the Thessalonians then, just as he does now! He is deeply proud of them.

This kind of profound affirmation is found elsewhere in Paul's letters (2 Cor. 1:14; Phil. 2:16; 4:1).

> **Relational Dynamic:** Again, we see Paul's deep love and affection for the Thessalonians! Without this genuine love, the church planter's work will be stunted – it will just be "ministry production."

20 For you are our glory and joy.

Repeats and thus emphasizes the previous verse with more force. Also this refers not to the future but to the present time. Paul has pride and joy in the Thessalonians now. They're doing well (1 Thess. 1:2-10)!

> **Fivefold Ministry:** The role of the fivefold ministries is to equip the people – to build their lives (see 1 Cor. 9:1, "Are not you my workmanship in the Lord?", and 1 Cor. 3:6-9). This was Paul's purpose. The people he built will be his glory and joy on the Last Day. His vision was not to build an enduring organization but people – the living Bride of Christ!

Chapter 3

3:1-5 THE SENDING OF TIMOTHY

1 Therefore when we could bear it no longer, we were willing to be left behind at Athens alone,

when we could bear it no longer

Paul knew the opposition toward him during his time there would have continued in his absence and been directed toward the Thessalonian believers.

Ever since his abrupt departure, he has wanted to know the state of their faith (1 Thess. 3:5) and also to have the opportunity to encourage them to endure.

willing to be left behind at Athens alone

The Greek word means "abandoned." Paul was working hard at Athens and would certainly have needed both personal company and help with the work. But the Thessalonians had a greater need for Timothy.

> **Fivefold Ministry:** As a servant leader, Paul put the needs of the people before his own.

Athens

Paul probably wrote this letter from Corinth. He was in Athens before then.

2 and we sent Timothy, our brother and God's co-worker in the Gospel of Christ, to establish and exhort you in your faith,

we sent Timothy

This is not mentioned in Acts. This was probably the decision of Paul, Timothy and Silas.

It appears that Paul had traveled from Berea to Athens without Timothy and Silas (Acts 17:14). When he reached Athens he sent a message back to Berea (by the Berean believers who had traveled with him) for Timothy and Silas to join him in Athens as soon as possible (Acts 17:15). Apparently Timothy and Silas did so. Then, from Athens, they sent Timothy to Thessalonica to see how the believers were doing and to encourage them. Silas also returned to Macedonia around the same time, perhaps to check on the Philippian church (Acts 18:5). Silas and Timothy both then returned from Macedonia to join Paul in Corinth where he had gone after Athens (Acts 18:1, 5). Then, from Corinth, Paul wrote this letter to the Thessalonians.

our brother

Another family reference. We also see how Paul spoke about his team members – not only affectionately but also highly, as peers.

God's co-worker

Every Christian leader is a co-worker with God (1 Cor. 3:9).

> **The Centrality of Christ:** Jesus is building His Church (Matt. 16:18). It is His work to be done in His way by His enabling and for His glory. It is not our work. We work in union with Him.

> **Fivefold Ministry:** True leaders do not set themselves up as celebrities, higher than others. Instead they build teams of co-workers – teams of affection, honor, respect and love (Rom. 16: 3, 9, 21; Phil. 2:25, Phm. 1, 24).

> **Relational Dynamic:** Paul had a healthy team culture that exemplified humility and mutual respect to the churches they planted. Culture is nurtured through the examples of the leaders and how they treat each other. If the leaders are competitive then the people will be competitive.

to establish and exhort you in your faith

The two verbs express that Timothy's purpose was to strengthen them by encouraging them.

your faith

The whole of their Christian life.

3 that no one be moved by these afflictions. For you yourselves know that we are destined for this.

that no one be moved by these afflictions

In the Parable of the Sower, Jesus taught that many who initially received the Word of God fell away after tribulation and persecution (Mark 4:17). Paul knows the Thessalonians are under pressure and he doesn't want that to happen to them.

moved

Shaken or disturbed.

you yourselves know that we are destined for this

Paul had taught them this. He prepared them for the inevitable suffering that would come. Therefore, they should not be disturbed now that it has come (1 Pet. 4:12-19).

we are destined for this

Every believer is called to suffer for Jesus in one way or another (John 15:19-21). Thus, the suffering was not only predicted, it is God's will for them. Moreover, it is a sign of His approval, not His displeasure.

4 For when we were with you, we kept telling you beforehand that we were to suffer affliction, just as it has come to pass, and just as you know.

we kept telling you beforehand ... just as it has come to pass

Paul told them it would happen and then it did. So they should not be surprised or shaken by it. It's the normal Christian experience.[16]

we kept telling you

Apparently Paul repeatedly taught about sufferings. He did not try to hide the difficult path that lay before the new church or make it seem any "friendlier" than what it really was. The New Testament Church was not a "seeker-friendly" church; they taught the truth clearly and deeply.

> **Instructional Dynamic:** Suffering was an important part of Paul's very earliest teaching to a newly-planted church. In addition, he continued to teach and exhort them about this all along (Acts 14:22).

---

16   The "Prosperity Gospel" that ravages the Church around the world by falsely promising a life of health, wealth and security to all who have faith, was not known in the Early Church.

5 For this reason, when I could bear it no longer, I sent to learn about your faith, for fear that somehow the tempter had tempted you and our labor would be in vain.

when I could bear it no longer

Paul's deep concern for his spiritual children. While he trusts the Holy Spirit for them, he still has this natural care.

I sent

We can see the inner dynamics of Paul's team. In verse 2, it is "we sent" – a corporate decision. Here it is "I sent" – Paul is still responsible.

to learn about your faith

Paul wants to see how they are doing – to be assured they are continuing to walk with God.

the tempter

This is the second time Satan is directly mentioned (1 Thess. 2:18).[17] The young church is living in a heavy battle – an adversary and a tempter is against her.

the tempter had tempted you

The specific temptation is to abandon their faith in order to avoid the sufferings. In fact, this is the ultimate goal of every temptation from Satan – that believers will abandon their faith. "The one who endures to the end will be saved" (Matt. 24:13).

---

[17] The word "tempter" only occurs twice in the New Testament. The other place is Matthew 4:3.

and our labor would be in vain

If the Thessalonians fall away, then Paul's work on their behalf will be in vain (Gal. 4:11; Phil. 2:16). Paul himself will still be rewarded by God for his labor (Is. 49:4; 1 Cor. 3:8), but the Thessalonians will be lost forever (Heb. 6:4-9; 10:39; 2 Pet. 2:20-22).

3:6-13 TIMOTHY'S REPORT AND PAUL'S RESPONSE AND PRAYER

6 But now that Timothy has come to us from you, and has brought us the good news of your faith and love and reported that you always remember us kindly and long to see us, as we long to see you –

But now

Before Timothy went, Paul was deeply concerned. But now that he has returned with such a good report, Paul is filled with joy.

Timothy has come to us from you

Silas had returned from Macedonia before Timothy (Acts 18:5) and is with Paul now. The Greek is "Timothy has just now come to us from you." Paul wrote this letter almost immediately upon Timothy's return.

your faith and love

They are doing well, standing strong with faith toward God and love toward each other (1 Thess. 1:3; 2 Thess. 1:3). They have not been shaken by the persecution.

you always remember us kindly and long to see us, as we long to see you

Just as Paul loves the Thessalonians and longs to see them, they also remember their spiritual father with great affection and long to see him again. Even though Paul, in one sense, has brought suffering to their lives, yet they know he's given them eternal truth.

Relational Dynamic: They affectionately remembered Paul's life, not just his ministry gifting or his teaching.

Fivefold Ministry: Often leaders focus on their gifting and ministry work, when it will be their lives that are actually remembered the most.

Timothy was sent to find out how they are doing. He returns to Paul to report that they are doing very well toward God and also toward Paul – they have not been led astray by Paul's opponents or shaken by the persecution.

7 for this reason, brothers, in all our distress and affliction we have been comforted about you through your faith.

for this reason

Timothy's good report has greatly comforted Paul in the midst of his own affliction.

distress and affliction

Possibly Paul indicates internal distress (anxiety, verse 5) by the first word and external affliction (persecution) by the second.

8 For now we live, if you are standing fast in the Lord.

we live

Paul and his team are refreshed, full of joy and enthusiasm (3 John 4). This shows the closeness of Paul's relationship with the

Thessalonians, that he is so personally affected by their condition. This is the spiritual reality of the Body of Christ (1 Cor. 12:26).

9 For what thanksgiving can we return to God for you, for all the joy that we feel for your sake before our God,

what thanksgiving can we return to God

How could we ever thank God enough? Paul is so filled with joy at the good report about the Thessalonians that he cannot express enough gratitude to God. He is overflowing with both joy and relief. He deeply cares about the Thessalonians.

> **Fivefold Ministry:** The true leader's very life is bound up in the people he serves (2 Cor. 11:28-29). It is not just a job that he is professionally responsible for. Moreover, the leader genuinely cares for his friends. He is not "over" them, aloof and detached.

thanksgiving ... to God

Paul did not take the credit for their growth. It came from God (1 Cor. 3:7; Phil. 2:13).

10 as we pray most earnestly night and day that we may see you face to face and supply what is lacking in your faith?

we pray most earnestly night and day

Paul and his team were very serious about prayer.

> **Fivefold Ministry:** Above all, the Christian leader will be a man or woman of prayer. Leaders are intercessors. Prayer is the source of their power – not marketing and social media.

that we may see you face to face

Even though they're doing so well, Paul still wants to return. He deeply cares about them and knows they have more to learn. The relationship of church planter to the church should be a lifelong one.

> **Relational Dynamic:** Jesus committed Himself to be with us until the end of the age (Matt. 28:20; Heb. 13:5). Similarly, it's healthy for the spiritual father to have a lifelong relationship with the churches he has planted.

supply what is lacking in your faith

Timothy had told Paul about how well the Thessalonians were doing, but would also have told him about some shortcomings in the church. In addition, the Thessalonians had likely asked for help on certain matters. In the second half of the letter, Paul will deal with some of these things, after having first given such strong affirmation and commendation to them.

Paul had an interdependent relationship with the churches he planted. He established them to be strong and able to stand on their own feet by God's grace. Their continued growth did not depend on him. At the same time, they were not independent of him. He continued to interact with them as much as he could, teaching, correcting and encouraging them.

> **Wider Church:** A healthy local church will have strong ongoing relationships with other churches and leaders, and especially with their own spiritual fathers and mothers.

supply

The Greek word is another form of the same word that is translated "equip" in Ephesians 4:12. It means to prepare, repair, restore, complete.

> **Fivefold Ministry:** The role of the leaders is to "equip" the saints to do the work of the ministry and thus build up the Body of Christ, not to do all the work themselves. Throughout this letter Paul addresses the "brothers" – meaning all the people there – and instructs them to do the work of the ministry.

what is lacking in your faith

As very young believers they have a lot to learn. In addition, there are specific corrections and input needed. They're doing well (1 Thess. 1:7), but they're not perfect.

While Paul can send letters like this one to help them, a personal visit will be much better (2 John 12).

11 Now may our God and Father Himself, and our Lord Jesus, direct our way to you,

our God and Father Himself, and our Lord Jesus, direct

This affirms the equality of the Father and the Son. There are two subjects here (God the Father and the Lord Jesus) but the verb ("direct") is singular. In other words, Paul says, in effect, "May He direct our way ..." rather than, "May They direct our way ..." Also the use of the word "Himself" emphasizes that it is God Himself with whom the Lord Jesus is One. Finally, the rest of the prayer is toward Jesus – Paul has easily transitioned from the Father to the Son as God, without any fear of polytheism. There is only one God (1 Cor. 8:6); yet the Father, Son and Holy Spirit are distinct and equal.

In verse 10, Paul spoke of the abundance and fervency of his prayer. Now he gives the content of his prayer – that he can go to them and that they will continue to grow in Christ.

In this prayer, he anticipates some of the specific issues he'll deal with in the remaining part of the letter. Paul moves from their love for one another (to be addressed in 1 Thess. 4:3-12) to what appears to be a major concern in the letter, some misunderstandings about the nature of Jesus' return (to be addressed in 1 Thess. 4:13-5:11).

direct our way to you

Satan has hindered him until now (1 Thess. 2:18), but Paul trusts that God will get him there. God had initially sent him to Macedonia (Acts 16:10) and Paul believes He will send him back. This prayer was not answered for a long time (Acts 20:1-2).

> **Spiritual Dynamic:** Church planting is a deeply spiritual thing. Paul was led by the Holy Spirit regarding where to go (and not go) and what to do. In addition, he always experienced intense spiritual warfare. Today's church planter and church leader must have both a strong life of prayer and a strong team of intercessors if he is to succeed.

12 and may the Lord make you increase and abound in love for one another and for all, as we do for you,

and for all

Love toward all people (Gal. 6:10). In a healthy church, every member will reach out to the lost.

as we do for you

Paul's teaching does not occur in a vacuum. He has first personally lived among them and exemplified the truth he then teaches. He has shown them what it means to love and serve others within the church and outside the church.

> **Relational Dynamic:** Our teaching must always have a context – our own lives and examples.

13 so that He may establish your hearts blameless in holiness before our God and Father, at the coming of our Lord Jesus with all His saints.

your hearts

Your inner life, will, motives, character. Paul's vision is for the building of the whole person.

blameless in holiness

The Bride for which Jesus returns will be spotless and without blemish (Eph. 5:27).

Love toward the brethren and holiness toward God are the two key things Paul prays for in verses 12-13. Paul then goes on in the following verses to deal with each of them. These two are the focus also of the entire book of 1 John: those who know God will walk in holiness and love their brethren. These are the two Great Commandments: love God and therefore obey Him, and love one another.

at the coming of our Lord Jesus with all His saints

"Saints" means "holy ones" and probably refers to the angels who will be with Jesus when He returns (Matt. 25:31; 2 Thess. 1:7).[18] Paul's words appear to be a reference to Zechariah 14:5: "Then the Lord my God will come, and all the holy ones with Him."[19]

---

18 It may also be a reference to the believers who have died already but will be resurrected at Jesus' return and caught up with the living believers to meet the Lord in the air (1 Thess. 4:13-17).

19 Most of the believers in Thessalonica were Gentiles; therefore, the letter contains very few references to the Old Testament, in contrast with others of Paul's letters like Romans or Galatians. Both letters to the Thessalonians do not assume much existing Old Testament familiarity. Other major Old Testament references are to the Day of the Lord (1 Thess. 5:1-3) and to the prophets of the Old Testament (1 Thess. 2:15).

Chapter 4

4:1-8 SEXUAL PURITY

1 Finally, then, brothers, we ask and urge you in the Lord Jesus, that as you received from us how you ought to walk and to please God, just as you are doing, that you do so more and more.

Finally

The Greek word indicates that Paul is changing subjects now. This does not mean, "in closing"; it is more like, "in the final section of this letter."

as you received from us

Paul already taught them these things when he was with them, but now he needs to repeat them.

It is often unrealistic for the leader to address matters one time and then expect them to be settled. The leader must continually, and patiently, return to the same issues again and again.

how you ought to walk and to please God

Paul had given very specific and practical instructions about how to live (1 Thess. 2:12).

and to please God

Our Christian lives are not slavish obedience to a set of rules. Instead we love God and desire to please Him.

just as you are doing, that you do so more and more

He affirms the Thessalonians for obeying his instructions, while encouraging them to do it more. This is a gentle way of leading into dealing with the issue of sexual purity.

2 For you know what instructions we gave you through the Lord Jesus.

For you know what instructions we gave you

Repeats and amplifies the previous verse.

> **Instructional Dynamic:** Apparently Paul had taught on sexual purity very early in the new church's life. One of the first things he wanted the new believers to learn was how to have victory over sexual sin.

instructions

The Greek word means "commands."

through the Lord Jesus

Paul appeals directly to Jesus' authority here, and is quite strict in the following verses (verses 6 and 8). Thus, sexual purity is an extremely important issue for the church. This was one of the things that was urged for the Gentiles in the letter from the Council in Jerusalem (Acts 15:20, 29).

3 For this is the will of God, your sanctification: that you abstain from sexual immorality;

the will of God

This is not man's recommendation but God's direct command.

sanctification

The Greek word is translated in the New Testament both as "holiness" and as "sanctification." The word literally means to be "set apart" or "consecrated."[20] As followers of the Lord Jesus, our lives must be set apart from sin and to God and, therefore, daily growing into His holy likeness.

---

20 The word "set apart ones" is used in the Old Testament of people consecrated or devoted to an idol as "cult prostitutes" (Deut. 23:17; 1 Kings 14:24; 15:12; etc.). In such cases, they were obviously not "holy" in any sense of moral purity. When we are consecrated to the infinitely holy God, however, moral holiness will result from consecration.

that you abstain from sexual immorality

A very important aspect of sanctification. In the Bible, sexual purity is a major issue. As former idolaters,[21] many of the Thessalonian believers would have had pasts that were steeped in immorality. Today, many people who come to Christ have sexual sin in their past and this must be directly addressed by the church leaders.

sexual immorality

The Greek word (*porneia*) is very broad and includes adultery, premarital and extramarital sex, prostitution, homosexuality, and other things. The Thessalonians lived in a pagan culture in which sexual immorality was not only practiced openly as a normal part of life but was also encouraged – especially among men.[22] This is why Paul repeatedly dealt with it in his letters.

4 that each one of you know how to control his own body in holiness and honor,

each one of you

Paul's purpose is for every member of the church to know God and walk in holiness.

control

The Greek word literally means to "acquire" or "gain." Here Paul probably means for someone to gain control of his own body, unlike the Gentiles who lack such self-control and are given over to lust (verse 5). Thus, it is possible for believers to walk in victory over

---

21 Idolatry, in biblical times, was usually heavily associated with sexual immorality.
22 For example, one Greek philosopher wrote, "Mistresses we keep for the sake of pleasure, concubines for the daily care of our persons, but wives to bear us legitimate children." (Demosthenes, *Against Neaera,* section 122)

sexual sin. We do not have to be bound by the things that bind the lost. Christians are not the helpless victims of their own passions or the culture around them.

body

The word is literally "vessel" – like a jar. The metaphor of man as a "vessel" is used numerous times in the New Testament (Rom. 9:21-23; 2 Tim. 2:20-21; 1 Pet. 3:7). Here it refers to the body (see also 2 Cor. 4:7).

honor

Sexual sin dishonors the people involved, the church and God Himself. But sex within marriage honors man and God (Heb. 13:4).

5 not in the passion of lust like the Gentiles who do not know God;

the Gentiles who do not know God

Not very long ago, many of the Thessalonian believers were such Gentiles but now they are contrasted with the Gentiles! Now they are part of God's family. Paul reminds them of their recent history but he does it in such a way as to encourage their distance and disassociation from it (1 Cor. 6:9-11).

who do not know God

God is holy; therefore, those who know God will not live in such lust (1 John 3:4-10).

In the Roman and Greek world, marital unfaithfulness on the part of husbands was not condemned. Paul, in stark contrast, severely condemned it.

6 that no one transgress and wrong his brother in this matter, because the Lord is an avenger in all these things, as we told you beforehand and solemnly warned you.

wrong his brother in this matter

Through committing adultery with his brother's wife.

It appears that the sin of adultery has occurred in the Thessalonian church. Paul originally had taught them against all sexual immorality when he was there. Then this sin of adultery happened after his departure. Timothy tells Paul about it. Now Paul repeats and sternly emphasizes his warning against it.

his brother

This heightens the sin – it is your brother you are wronging!

the Lord is an avenger in all these things

God will punish this sin (Eph. 5:5-6; Col. 3:5-6; Gal. 5:21; 6:7-8).

as we told you beforehand and solemnly warned you

When Paul was with them, he taught clearly and seriously about this.

> **Instructional Dynamic:** Paul taught very sternly about sexual sin to new believers. This is not an "advanced truth" that should be reserved for the mature. The Thessalonians were surrounded by paganism – as we are today – and they needed to be clearly taught and warned against the soul-destroying immorality that was so deeply a part of it.

7 For God has not called us for impurity, but in holiness.

not ... for impurity, but in holiness

God's purpose for His people (Eph. 2:10). This stands in contrast to their former lives of impurity and idolatry.

8 Therefore whoever disregards this, disregards not man but God, who gives His Holy Spirit to you.

disregards not man but God

A strong warning: if you reject this teaching you have rejected God! This also indicates that originally God had specifically directed Paul to teach sexual purity to the new believers, and now He inspires him to repeat this warning to them in view of the existing sin or sins in their midst.

who gives His Holy Spirit to you

First, because our bodies are the temples of the Holy Spirit, therefore we must be holy in our bodies (1 Cor. 6:12-20). Second, the Holy Spirit in us will give us the power to overcome sin (Rom. 8:13).

If 1 Thessalonians was the first book written by Paul, then this is his first mention of the *gift* of the Holy Spirit – in the context of sexual immorality. God gives us His Holy Spirit to transform our lives!

> **Spiritual Dynamic:** Paul shows the need for dependence upon the Holy Spirit. This is a very positive encouragement to them, that the Holy Spirit will empower their transformed lives.

4:9-12 BROTHERLY LOVE AND PERSONAL RESPONSIBILITY

9 Now concerning brotherly love you have no need for anyone to write to you, for you yourselves have been taught by God to love one another,

brotherly love

In contrast to sexual immorality.

taught by God

The direct work of the Holy Spirit in their hearts, convicting and leading them (John 16:13; 1 John 2:27). In a healthy church, every member is directly connected to Christ. He is the One who builds our lives.

> **Spiritual Dynamic:** Clearly when Paul was with them, he did not give them a mere moral code or a list of ethical demands. The truth of God for them was a life transformed by inward union with Christ, with the Risen Lord living His life through each one by His great grace (1 Thess. 5:22-24). It is God who works in us both to will and to do His good pleasure (Phil. 2:13).

10 for that indeed is what you are doing to all the brothers throughout Macedonia. But we urge you, brothers, to do this more and more,

all the brothers throughout Macedonia

The Thessalonians had extensive relationships all over the entire province (1 Thess. 1:7)!

Thessalonica was the capital city of the province of Macedonia. Therefore, the believers would have shown their love and provided hospitality to the brothers from other places when those brothers came to the capital. They could also have given help of various kinds to churches in other towns. At every opportunity, the Thessalonian believers served many others outside of their own local church.

Paul later commended the believers in Macedonia for their great generosity (2 Cor. 8:1-5).

> **Wider Church:** From the beginning the Thessalonians interacted in a variety of ways with the other churches in their region. Paul established this culture.

you are doing ... do this more and more

Love is something we do – it is not just a feeling or words (1 John 3:16-18). If we love one another then we will serve one another – the second facet of the Healthy Church Model.

> **Instructional Dynamic:** Paul warmly affirms what they're already doing while urging them to do more. His teaching is very positive. He does not merely point out the need for improvement. Paul was always looking for things to affirm!

11 and to aspire to live quietly, and to mind your own affairs, and to work with your hands, as we instructed you,

And ... live quietly ... mind your own affairs ... work with your hands

This is another way to show brotherly love – or at least it's a way to not abuse brotherly love!

It is possible that Timothy told Paul about some abuses along these lines. Paul mentions it later in 1 Thessalonians 5:14.

live quietly

In the sense of orderly and peaceably. "Mind your own business and earn your own living." These two are closely connected. Paul addresses this again in 2 Thessalonians. People who are not working have the time to be busy-bodies (2 Thess. 3:11-12).

work with your hands

The typical Greek attitude at the time was that slaves did the manual labor. In contrast, Paul honors those who work with their hands.

The point is not that the believers are to do only manual work, but that they were to earn their own living instead of asking other believers or the church to support them.

It's possible that some were so focused on Jesus' imminent return that they neglected their own practical responsibilities and found it easier to simply depend on others to provide for them.

Paul certainly believed in Jesus' imminent return – he teaches this just a few verses later in verse 17 – but he still taught the saints to live their lives with a long-term perspective. Both time frames are side-by-side here.

Moreover, Paul shows here that all work is glorifying to God and appropriate for believers – not just "sacred" work (Eph. 6:5-9).

as we instructed you

Paul not only instructed them to do this. He also modeled this (1 Thess. 2:9; Acts 20:33-35).

> **Instructional Dynamic:** This was part of Paul's initial teaching to a new church.

12 so that you may walk properly before outsiders and be dependent on no one.

outsiders

Unbelievers. Effective outreach demands that our lives are not offensive to those we're hoping to reach.

The life and testimony of a church is a witness to the watching world (Matt. 5:14-16; Col. 4:5-6), and it is one of the ways the world is drawn to Jesus. They see that we are different and they want to enjoy that shared love of the family of God.

be dependent on no one

In addition, be able to give generously to others in genuine need (Eph. 4:28).

Paul has two purposes here: that they live in a way that earns favor with unbelievers and that they are not financially dependent on others. This was the personal example Paul had set for them (1 Thess. 2:9). This was not a promotion of individualism and complete independence from others in the church, but rather personal responsibility.

> **Instructional Dynamic:** In Paul's first teaching to a new church, he taught the need for every member to reach out to unbelievers by their actions as well as their words.

Apparently, Paul's instructions here did not solve the problem and Paul, a short time later, had to very sternly admonish them about this in 2 Thessalonians 3:6-12.[23]

---

[23] Paul's two letters to the Thessalonians may have only been a few weeks apart. They are closely connected. The second letter is written to explain the right application of the issues brought up in the first.

4:13-18 BELIEVERS WHO HAVE DIED

13 But we do not want you to be uninformed, brothers, about those who are asleep, that you may not grieve as others do who have no hope.

uninformed

It appears that the Thessalonians were distressed at the thought of separation from their departed brethren, and were unclear about their future as it related to Jesus' return and the resurrection. Probably this was a question or issue that Timothy brought back to Paul.

This is the classic passage in the Bible on the rapture of the church.

This is the first and only matter in this letter on which the Thessalonians are receiving instruction from Paul for the first time. Everywhere else in the letter, Paul uses language indicating it is a reminder. Paul was only with them for a short time; he did not have sufficient time to teach them everything!

those who are asleep

Believers who have died (John 11:11-14; Acts 13:36; 1 Cor. 15:6, 18, 20, 51).

The image of sleeping does not promote the false doctrine of "soul sleep" which says that dead believers are in an unconscious state while they await the resurrection.[24]

---

[24] This is taught by Unitarians, Universalists, the Seventh-Day Adventist Church and the Jehovah's Witnesses.

In the Bible, "sleeping" describes the physical body which appears to be asleep.[25] Moreover, sleep is used as a metaphor to describe rest from one's labor and that death is temporary in the same manner that sleep is temporary. Finally, "sleep" is a euphemism that tempers the stark reality of death.

The biblical teaching is that believers are fully conscious with Christ in heaven after death (Ps. 16:11; 73:24; Luke 23:43; 2 Cor. 5:8; Phil. 1:21-23; Heb. 12:23).

> **Instructional Dynamic:** Paul taught about life after death (for believers and unbelievers) to the new church.

that you may not grieve as others do

Paul is not suggesting that Christians should not grieve the death of believers. Of course they will (Acts 8:2), but they will not grieve *as* others do.

others

The Greek is "the rest"; besides Christians, the entire world is lost.

others ... who have no hope

The unsaved. They are "without hope and without God in the world" (Eph. 2:12).

hope

Believers have tremendous hope for the future after death: hope that their bodies will be resurrected, hope that they will be with Christ

---

25   The Greeks and Romans also used this figure of sleep for death. We use the same figure of speech today: the word "cemetery" means a sleeping-place.

after death, hope of seeing deceased friends and family again, hope of a future glorious life, hope of eternal union with God!

14 For since we believe that Jesus died and rose again, even so, through Jesus, God will bring with Him those who have fallen asleep.

since … even so

Our future resurrection is based on the reality of Jesus' resurrection. He was the "Firstfruits" (1 Cor. 15:20) and "Firstborn" (Col. 1:18) from the dead. The fact of His resurrection provides us with the certainty of our own (John 14:19; Rom. 6:4; 1 Cor. 6:14; 2 Cor. 4:14).

those who have fallen asleep

All the saved who have died before Jesus' return.

God will bring with Him those who have fallen asleep

Their souls will return from heaven and be reunited with their bodies that are resurrected.

> **Instructional Dynamic:** Paul taught Jesus' death, resurrection and Second Coming to new believers, as well as the future resurrection of our bodies.

15 For this we declare to you by a Word from the Lord, that we who are alive, who are left until the coming of the Lord, will not precede those who have fallen asleep.

by a Word from the Lord

Paul received this doctrine by direct prophetic revelation from God (2 Cor. 12:1-4).

we who are alive

At this point in his life, Paul believed that Jesus was returning so soon that he would be alive to see it (1 Cor. 15:51; Phil. 3:21). Later, near the end of his life, he knew he would not be alive for Jesus' return (2 Tim. 4:6).

Every generation should expect that the Lord could return at any time. All of us should be living in hope of the imminent return of our Savior (2 Pet. 3:3-13). Then we will live in the fear of God, and be very aggressive regarding evangelism, church planting and making disciples. We will not fall asleep or be complacent as the foolish virgins were (Matt. 26:1-13).

At the same time, we should also think and plan with a long-term perspective, as Paul instructs the Thessalonians in verses 11-12, rather than giving up on the practical things of life because Jesus is coming back today! Both perspectives are taught side-by-side here.

will not precede

The living believers will not go before those who have died. In fact, "the dead in Christ will rise first" and then we will all be resurrected and participate in Jesus' glory (verses 16-17).

16 For the Lord Himself will descend from heaven with a cry of command, with the voice of an archangel, and with the sound of the trumpet of God. And the dead in Christ will rise first.

the Lord Himself

Jesus Himself will return bodily.[26] The Greek is emphatic – it is the Lord Himself (Acts 1:11).

> **Instructional Dynamic:** Paul taught the new church about Jesus' imminent *bodily* return.

with a cry of command

The Lord shouts a command – perhaps for the dead to awaken or to the angels with Him. The Greek means a "signal shout" or "war shout."

with the voice of an archangel

The archangel shouts a command. This is possibly Michael who is named as an archangel in Jude 9.[27] Others associate this angel with Gabriel since he also announced the events of the first coming of Jesus (Luke 1:19-20, 26-38).

with the sound of the trumpet of God

A trumpet blast often accompanies great manifestations of God's glory (Ex. 19:16; Ps. 47:5). Trumpets are connected with many events

---

[26] This directly contradicts the false teaching that says that Jesus will return spiritually in His mature church.
[27] Michael is also mentioned in Dan. 10:13, 21; 12:1; Rev. 12:7. "Archangels" are not mentioned at all in the Old Testament, but they are in intertestamental Judaism. It's possible that Gabriel is also an archangel.

of the Last Days (Rev. 8 – 9). Here the trumpet heralds Jesus' return (Zech. 9:14; Matt. 24:31; 1 Cor. 15:52).

We don't know whether these three events will happen sequentially or simultaneously. However, we do know it will be dramatic!

the dead in Christ will rise first

Their bodies will be resurrected. This resurrection is only for believers – those "in Christ." Unbelievers will be resurrected later and stand before the final judgment of the Great White Throne (Rev. 20:12-13).

17 Then we who are alive, who are left, will be caught up together with them in the clouds to meet the Lord in the air, and so we will always be with the Lord.

we who are alive

Again Paul says "we." Every generation should be looking for Jesus' imminent return.

will be caught up together with them

First the dead in Christ are raised from the dead with new glorified bodies. Then believers who are alive will be "changed" (1 Cor. 15:50-55; Phil. 3:21) and have glorified bodies also. Then all of us will rise together and meet the Lord in the air. This is the "rapture" (Matt. 24:31).

together with them

One body. Jesus has one glorious Church comprised of all the saints of all time. What a day that will be!

caught up

The Greek word could be translated "seized" or "snatched." It carries the idea that this happens suddenly and swiftly, and is accomplished vehemently and by great power.

In Latin the word for "caught up" is *rapturo*, from which comes the term "rapture." Thus, while the English word "rapture" is not found in the Bible, the idea itself is here.[28]

in the clouds

Jesus was taken up in a cloud (Acts 1:9) and will return with clouds (Rev. 1:7; Dan. 7:13).

meet the Lord in the air

Paul is not explicit here whether the Lord continues on to the earth (post-tribulation rapture) or goes back to heaven for a time (pre-tribulation and mid-tribulation raptures). What Paul is explicit about is that we will meet the Lord and then always be with Him! We look forward to this time when we are "gathered together to Him" (2 Thess. 2:1). To be present with the Lord is our great hope (John 14:3).

the air

The heavens around the earth (Eph. 2:2). Thus, Jesus descends from the highest heavens (verse 16; the spiritual realm of the "third heaven" of 2 Cor. 12:2) and meets His people in the lower heavens or the atmosphere around the earth.

---

28 The word actually does appear in the Latin Vulgate (a late-4th century Latin translation of the Bible): *rapiemur*, from the Latin verb *rapio* meaning "to catch up" or "take away."

we will always be with the Lord

The rest of the events of the Last Days are simply not mentioned here. Whatever happens next, we will be with the Lord – forever!

18 Therefore encourage one another with these words.

Therefore

In contrast to the massive volume of eschatological speculation on this passage, it must be clearly understood that Paul's purpose here is not to establish a detailed doctrine about the timing of the rapture and all the events of the Last Days, but rather to encourage the Thessalonians in the midst of their persecution.

with these words

The hope of Jesus' imminent return (Tit. 2:13) and then our eternity with Him is our single greatest encouragement in the midst of our sufferings here. These words are just as much a comfort to us today as they were to the Thessalonians.

Chapter 5

5:1-3 THE DAY OF THE LORD AND THE UNBELIEVERS

---

1 Now concerning the times and the seasons, brothers, you have no need to have anything written to you.

the times and the seasons

This is a figure of speech meaning a specific time. Essentially, Paul is saying, "You know the hour in which we live – the time of the end is soon!"

you have no need to have anything written to you

Paul had already taught them clearly about the Day of the Lord.

2 For you yourselves are fully aware that the Day of the Lord will come like a thief in the night.

fully aware

Apparently this was a major part of Paul's teaching to a new church.

the Day of the Lord

In the Old Testament, the expression "Day of the Lord" occurs eighteen times in the prophets (e.g., Joel 3:14-17; Amos 5:18-20; Ob. 15; Zeph. 1:7; Mal. 4:5). A similar expression, "on that Day," occurs more than 200 times in the Old Testament. In the New Testament there are similar expressions, such as "Day of Jesus Christ" (1 Cor. 1:8; 2 Cor. 1:14; Phil. 1:6, 10; 2 Peter 3:10, 12). "Day of the Lord" appears here and in 2 Thessalonians 2:2.

The "Day of the Lord" is not a single day but a period of time that includes all the judgments of God upon humanity, Jesus' return, the deliverance of God's people, the restoration of Israel, and the establishment of God's Kingdom on the earth.

like a thief in the night

This means it will be unexpected and that many, perhaps most, will be unprepared (Matt. 24:36-51; Luke 17:20-32; 2 Pet. 3:10; Rev. 3:3; 16:15). Moreover, it indicates the terrible result of that Day for many.

> **Instructional Dynamic:** Paul had taught them the main elements of the coming Day of the Lord.

3 While people are saying, "There is peace and security," then sudden destruction will come upon them as labor pains come upon a pregnant woman, and they will not escape.

peace and security

The world thinks that everything is fine, but judgment is about to fall at the moment when they least expect it.[29]

This may also refer to false prophets among God's people, who proclaim peace in a time of judgment and lead the people into spiritual dullness (Ezek. 13:10).

as labor pains come upon a pregnant woman

The comparison here is that it will be both sudden and inescapable. Labor pains are a common biblical image of pain and destruction (e.g., Jer. 4:31).

they will not escape

The rich, the poor, the great, the lowly, the famous, the unknown – none will escape!

---

[29] The Roman emperors claimed to have established peace and security (Latin: *pax et securitas*) throughout the empire. Teachings like this along with the insistence that Jesus is Lord and God (at the time, Caesar was both lord and god to the Romans) would have sounded somewhat politically subversive and may have contributed to the persecution against Paul and the young believers (Acts 17:7). Romans could understandably interpret proclaiming another king as treason against the emperor. Roman citizens pledged complete loyalty to Caesar, and Thessalonica's devotion to the imperial cult made this a religious matter as well. Thessalonica had a temple for the worship of the emperor and its coins honored Julius and Augustus Caesar as gods.

5:4-11 THE DAY OF THE LORD AND THE BELIEVERS

4 But you are not in darkness, brothers, for that day to surprise you like a thief.

But you

Believers may not know the exact day, but we do know "the times and the seasons." We are in the Last Days and must remain ready at all times!

in darkness

Believers are in neither ignorance nor moral darkness.

surprise

The Greek word means "to catch, seize or overcome." Those who live in darkness will be surprised when the end comes.

like a thief

That Day will not surprise you as a thief surprises the homeowner.

5 For you are all children of light, children of the day. We are not of the night or of the darkness.

For you are all

All believers are called to know God, to walk in holiness and to always be ready for the Day of the Lord. Christians live in a completely different sphere of life from non-Christians.

children

The Greek is "sons" both times. "Son of" is a Hebrew expression signifying the same nature or character (e.g., Luke 16:8).

children of light

Light signifies righteousness, purity, truth.

children of the day

As opposed to the darkness of the night in which the unsaved have their being. We are to be different (2 Cor. 4:2-6; 6:14).

6 So then let us not sleep, as others do, but let us keep awake and be sober.

So then

Because you are of God, therefore you must live like it (Eph. 5:8)!

sleep

A figure of speech for being unaware of and indifferent to the things of God – unconcerned and unprepared for the Day.

others

The Greek is, "the rest" – the unsaved (1 Thess. 4:13). The rest of the world is in ignorance and moral slumber.

keep awake and be sober

Spiritually alert, self-controlled, prepared and ready.

7 For those who sleep, sleep at night, and those who get drunk, are drunk at night.

those who sleep … those who get drunk

The unsaved lived in a way that is natural for them. But you are followers of Jesus – therefore, your lives must be different!

8 But since we belong to the day, let us be sober, having put on the breastplate of faith and love, and for a helmet the hope of salvation.

we belong to the day

We are God's and possess His nature. So we must live like it.

sober

Repeats the word from verse 6.

having put on

For us, the night is over. We are now in the light; we belong to the day. Therefore, we need to put on the appropriate clothes for the day (Rom. 13:12-14).

the breastplate of faith and love

The breastplate consists of faith and love. This is our spiritual armor – faith toward God and love toward the brethren.

a helmet the hope of salvation

Our helmet is our hope of the imminent return of the Lord Jesus and our eternal salvation.

Our armor protects us. It's not enough to be awake and watchful; we also need to be guarded.

Unlike the world, who need physical armor, our protection is in knowing God, obeying Him and living out of His indwelling life (Eph. 6:10-18).

Paul mentions the three great virtues again: faith, love and hope (1 Thess. 1:3; 1 Cor. 13:13).

9 For God has not destined us for wrath, but to obtain salvation through our Lord Jesus Christ,

For

We should hope for our future eternal salvation because God has destined us for this and He is faithful to bring it to pass.

not destined us for wrath

In the context here, this refers to God's judgments of the Day of the Lord.

wrath

God's righteous punishment of the sin of man.

obtain salvation through our Lord Jesus Christ

Through our union with Christ, and on the basis of His death and resurrection on our behalf, we will inherit eternal salvation. Although we are saved now, salvation will be finally complete after the resurrection (Rom. 8:23; Eph. 1:14).

The Day of the Lord does not pose a threat to believers. Nevertheless, we must stay awake and sober.

10 who died for us so that whether we are awake or asleep we might live with Him.

whether we are awake or asleep

Whether we are alive or dead (1 Thess. 4:14) when He returns, our eternal state will be the same – life with Him!

Life or death makes no difference to the Christian's eternal union and fellowship with Jesus (Rom. 14:7-9).

11 Therefore encourage one another and build one another up, just as you are doing.

Therefore encourage one another

Paul again tells us what his primary purpose is in teaching these things: the comfort and encouragement of the saints (1 Thess. 4:18). His interest is not so much in delving into comprehensive and precise eschatological details. Paul's teaching was always practical, and it always had immediate relevance and application. He never taught theory for its own sake.

> **Instructional Dynamic:** Paul never lays out a systematic eschatological system like people do today with charts and timetables. He taught that there is a rapture coming but not the exact timing or precise order of events. His teaching always focused on building people's lives, rather than establishing elaborate doctrinal systems that have no practical benefit and usually serve to distract and divide God's people.

build one another up

In a healthy church, every member takes responsibility to build each other up to maturity. This building will occur as they encourage each other to stay awake, watching in hope for Jesus' return.

just as you are doing

This was the culture Paul had established from the beginning in this new church.

Relational Dynamic: Consistently, Paul is so careful to recognize the good things they're doing, even while exhorting them to further efforts.

5:12-13 LEADERS IN THE CHURCH

12 We ask you, brothers, to respect those who labor among you and are over you in the Lord and admonish you,

We ask you

Leaders usually will not ask people to respect them. It's appropriate for the spiritual father – in this case Paul, the one who planted the church – to ask on their behalf.

Thus, Paul instructs them: you are to build up one another (verse 11), and you are to build up your leaders (verses 12-13).

Through recognizing these leaders himself and asking the people to recognize them, in a sense Paul is visibly passing on the mantle of leadership from himself to these leaders. He is empowering them. A healthy church will have her own local leaders and will not be dependent on outsiders.

brothers

This means all the believers. It's the responsibility of all the members in the church to respect, love and care for their leaders. The leaders need care just as much as anyone else! Sadly, they often do not get it.

respect

The Greek word means to "know." In this context, it means that the saints are to recognize, appreciate and respect their leaders.[30]

---

[30] Some scholars have suggested that the leaders at Thessalonica were those who had status and wealth in the community, since this was the way leadership in the Diaspora synagogues emerged and it reflects the hierarchical character of Greco-Roman society. However, the way Paul speaks about the leaders here does not indicate that these leaders

those who labor among you

These are the leaders – those who labor. The Greek word means "hard labor" or "working to the point of weariness." They served the church because they loved the people, not for personal gain, and they worked very hard.

It's unlikely that these leaders were paid, but would have had full-time jobs outside of the church, like the majority of frontline church leaders in the world today. At the same time, there was not only a single "pastor" here but a number of people ("those who labor") working together (Phil. 1:1). In addition, the people and not a single pastor did the ministry work itself (Eph. 4:12); thus, it was sustainable.

Moreover, these leaders are "among you." Like Paul, who lived and served "in the middle of" the people (1 Thess. 2:7), these leaders did not show up once a week to stand on a stage and give a brief public performance to an "audience." They lived among the people, deeply engaged with them in the midst of their daily lives, serving them, working hard to equip them and guide them.

Finally, these leaders were laboring hard among the people – not among the programs. They weren't religious professionals running organizational programs. They equipped the people. It was close work, personal work, intense work. They did not function from an office; they labored in the homes of the people and in the marketplace. They were "among" them.

---

have existing status and recognition. In addition, the basis for them being recognized as leaders is specifically stated as being their work (1 Thess. 5:13) and not their social status.

Relational Dynamic: The new leaders in Thessalonica had not graduated from Bible school. In fact, they had never been to a single leadership class. They simply did what they had seen Paul do. That was how these leaders were trained – through time with Paul, as Paul taught them by his word and by his example, prayed with them and for them, gave them responsibilities and assignments, and so forth (see Mark 3:14-15). No doubt Timothy spent further time with them doing the same things when he was there.

The Leaders Equip the People: The role of the leaders is to equip the people to function in the work of the ministry and build up the church. To "equip" means to do whatever is necessary to nurture a daily life and culture in which every member functions properly (Eph. 4:12). Since these leaders in Thessalonica had only been believers themselves for a few months, it is clear that their "equipping" work was not teaching academic courses! Rather they engaged deeply in the lives of the people, praying with them, encouraging them, serving them, and empowering them to take responsibility in the life of the church. In that rich context they would have taught and admonished them using the practical teaching they had heard from Paul and then Timothy.

are over you in the Lord

The Greek word means to "guide," "direct," "lead"; literally, "those who stand in front of you." The same word is used in 1 Timothy 5:17 of the elders who "rule" well, in Romans 12:8 of the one who "leads," and in 1 Timothy 3:4 and 12 of the elders and deacons who "manage" their households well.

Sometimes people will say that there is no mention of "leaders" in the New Testament and they are offended by any distinguishing of leaders from the rest of the people of God. The reality is that while all believers are one in Christ (Gal. 3:26-28), this distinction is made numerous times in the New Testament, as it is clearly made here (see also Phil. 1:1; 1 Tim. 3:1-13; 5:17; Tit. 1:5-9; Heb. 13:7, 17, 24; 1 Pet. 5:1-4; Acts 14:23; 20:28).

At the same time, Paul is not using the term here to describe an official position in the church.[31]

The Thessalonian church is only months old at this point and didn't yet have appointed leaders (such as in Acts 14:23 or Titus 1:5). Yet there are some here who are informally doing the work. Paul would have seen this beginning when he was there, and Timothy would have seen it in a little more advanced state and told Paul about them. Now Paul points them out to the people, but not by title or even by name. The people know who they are – they are serving the people, equipping the people, protecting the people, guiding the people. They are doing the work – not because they have a pastoral job or title but because they love the people and take responsibility and initiative.[32] It is natural and organic.

This is how Paul understands "leaders." Leaders are those who fulfill the functions of leadership – they are actually doing the hard daily "labor" of leading the people – rather than people with positions and titles.

---

31 "The position of προϊσταμένους ["over"] in 1 Thess. 5:12 between κοπιῶντας ["labor"] and νουθετοῦντας ["admonish"] (cf. Rom 12:8), combined with the general usage of the verb in the New Testament, makes it practically certain that the word cannot be a technical term of office, even if the persons referred to are office-bearers of the Church. This is further borne out by the wide and varied applications of the verb in the ordinary language of the time." (Moulton, J. H., & Milligan, G. (1930). *The Vocabulary of the Greek Testament* (p. 541). London: Hodder and Stoughton.)

32 Moreover, what qualified these leaders was not a formal degree but their lives in Christ, their character, servanthood and vision, and their initiative in guiding and equipping the people.

> **Fivefold Ministry:** We should think of the fivefold ministries and leadership itself not only as formal ministry "offices" but also as functions in the life of every local church.

The leaders here do not have formal titles, positions or religious jobs, and Paul tells the people to know them, recognize them and respect them. True leaders will do the work of leadership, with or without the recognition, but it's easier and better for everyone if they are "known" by the people (Heb. 13:17).

Moreover, this shows us how leaders are established in the Body of Christ. They are the ones who are actually doing the work. They take responsibility and initiative. They think and act in a way that serves and builds the life of the church. They do the work first and are identified and recognized later.[33]

in the Lord

These are spiritual leaders, who lead the Bride of Christ. They are not corporate leaders running a high-powered organization.

admonish you

This is part of the work of the leaders: to admonish or warn. Paul could have said "instruct" but he chose a certain kind of instruction. Apparently there are specific issues that are being dealt with there.

Thus, Paul says three things about the leaders. First, they "labor among you" – this generally describes their hard work on behalf of the people. Second, they "are over you" – this describes their guiding and directing of the people. Third, they "admonish you" – this is their teaching and equipping work (Eph. 4:12).

---

33   This is probably what happened in Acts 14:23 and Titus 1:5. Those who Paul appointed as the new elders in the churches were the ones who had already been doing the work and were recognized by the people (see also 1 Cor. 16:15-16).

In summary, in a healthy church, the leaders work hard at directing (overall leadership) and equipping, while the people do the actual work of the ministry and build up the Body of Christ (Eph. 4:12). Throughout the letter, it is the people that Paul exhorts to do the ministry work, not the leaders.[34]

13 and to esteem them very highly in love because of their work. Be at peace among yourselves.

very highly

The Greek is "exceeding abundantly" (1 Tim. 5:17). Paul wants the leaders to be deeply loved and respected by the people. Leadership is hard work, often without reward. In a healthy church the people will take care of their leaders as fellow believers and dear family members.

in love

The leaders are not separate and distant from the people and to be feared. They are to be respected in love. There should be a close, personal, mutually-loving relationship between the leaders and the people. Moreover, this love will be expressed in actions of love toward the leaders.

The leaders are to be known, recognized and appreciated, and esteemed and loved.

---

[34] "Brothers" stands for all the people in the church and is used many times in this letter in the context of Paul's instructions for them to do the various works of the ministry. He used this term fifteen times in 1 Thessalonians (1:4; 2:1, 9, 17; 3:7; 4:1, 10, 13; 5:1, 4, 12, 14, 25-27), and seven times in 2 Thessalonians (1:3; 2:1, 13, 15; 3:1, 6, 13).

because of their work

Sometimes leaders demand respect on the basis of their position or title, or their gifting, or even their own personality or charisma. Paul says respect should be given on the basis of the work they do. Leadership is not primarily a position but a responsibility. The Pharisees enjoyed the "positional" benefits of their leadership (Matt. 23:6) without actually serving the people (Matt. 23:4) and Jesus pronounced severe judgment against them (Matt. 23:33).

In Paul's understanding, the leaders do the work. They do not necessarily have a title. And they have no sense of personal entitlement or privilege because they are leaders. They are servant leaders who simply do the hard work, leading and equipping God's people so that they, the people, can do the work of the ministry. This is perfectly consistent with Jesus' teaching on leadership in Matthew 20:25-28. The leadership of the Kingdom is not the same as the leadership of the world!

> **Structure and Life:** From verses 12-13 we can see how Paul thought about organizational structure in the churches. He was not concerned that each church should adopt certain structural forms. Each local church was self-governing; there was no precisely-defined order imposed on them from central headquarters. In the Thessalonian church, Paul was not trying to fill particular set roles. Rather his focus was always on nurturing life. Then he would recognize the life that was happening, and then let that life take whatever structural form was most appropriate and helpful for supporting and sustaining the life.

Amazingly, in just these two verses, Paul has given us a clear picture of his understanding of leadership, the specific things that leaders do, the heart and character of leaders, and how leaders are established in new churches!

Be at peace among yourselves.

When the people disrespect their leaders, strife and division within the church will usually result. Healthy leaders who have a healthy relationship with the people will provide a tremendous basis for strong church unity.

5:14-18 EXHORTATIONS TOWARD EACH OTHER AND TOWARD GOD

14 And we urge you, brothers, admonish the idle, encourage the fainthearted, help the weak, be patient with them all.

brothers

Every member needs to take personal responsibility to build others in the church (1 Thess. 4:18; 5:11, 14; Rom. 15:2, 14; 1 Cor. 14:26; Col. 3:16; Heb. 10:24) – not only the leaders of verses 12-13.

> **Experiential Dynamic:** The church will grow to maturity not as new programs are initiated but as all the believers take responsibility to build each other's lives.

admonish the idle

Paul mentions this issue again (1 Thess. 4:11-12). It is the responsibility of the people in the church to correct this – not just the leaders. When Paul more sternly addresses the issue in 2 Thessalonians 3:6-15, it is again the responsibility of the people to take care of this problem.

the fainthearted

Perhaps refers to those who are intimidated by the persecution.

the weak

Those who are weak in their faith (Rom. 14:1).

be patient with them all

Not everyone in the church is strong. Those who are strong must not be impatient and frustrated with the weak and demand that they quickly achieve a high level of spirituality. Instead they must gently care for them (Rom. 14:1 – 15:7).

In addition, those who walk with God must be patient toward all men (1 Cor. 13:4; Gal. 5:22).

15 See that no one repays anyone evil for evil, but always seek to do good to one another and to everyone.

no one repays anyone evil for evil

Following Jesus' teachings in the Sermon on the Mount (Matt. 5:38-48; Rom. 12:17).

always seek to do good to one another and to everyone

This is a lifestyle of generosity. It is the very best way to overcome our inherent tendency to repay evil for evil. The Thessalonians, and others in Macedonia, seemed to learn this well (2 Cor. 8:1-5)!

and to everyone

To the lost. Every member in the church has the responsibility to reach out – not only with the words of the Gospel but with their good works (1 Thess. 3:12; Gal. 6:10; Matt. 5:13-16)

16 Rejoice always,

always

This is a command from Paul. In the midst of harsh circumstances, the Thessalonians should deliberately rejoice.

Our joy is not dependent on circumstances but on the reality that we're in Christ for eternity! Therefore, we can always rejoice (Phil. 3:1; 4:4).

17 pray without ceasing,

without ceasing

Constant inward fellowship with God and regular outward prayer. A life of continual dependence on God.

> **Spiritual Dynamic:** The life of the churches in Acts was bathed in prayer.

18 give thanks in all circumstances; for this is the will of God in Christ Jesus for you.

in all circumstances

Even in negative circumstances we can give thanks to God for His many blessings to us (Eph. 5:20). In addition, we can be thankful for His purposes in us and others that He will accomplish through the negative circumstances.

this is the will of God

It's very important to God that we choose to be continually grateful (Eph. 5:20). This is not just good advice from Paul – it is the specific will of God for every believer.

This is a beautiful unified instruction in verses 16-18. Whatever happens, continually be joyful, continually pray, and continually give thanks! This is a powerful lifestyle for the believer.

> **Experiential Dynamic:** When we go through sufferings, the sufferings themselves cannot hurt us or help us. It is how we respond that determines the impact of the sufferings on our lives. Paul gives a beautiful path here to do well through sufferings of every kind.

5:19-22 THE GIFTS OF THE HOLY SPIRIT

19 Do not quench the Spirit.

quench

The Greek word means "extinguish" or "put out," as of a fire. Figuratively it means to hinder or thwart.

the Spirit

It is His church and He wants to move, express Himself and speak in His church. There are so many ways the Holy Spirit can move, including the gifts of the Spirit (1 Cor. 12:1-11).

But Paul's exhortation to allow the Holy Spirit to move freely does not mean that the people should accept whatever happened or was said without discernment, as he shows in the next three verses.

20 Do not despise prophecies,

prophecies

The gift of prophecy was present in the new church at Thessalonica; it was part of the normal life of the church. Apparently there was a lot of abuse – as there is today – so it is necessary for Paul to say this. Perhaps Timothy had reported to Paul about some specific spiritual excesses and imbalances.

Spiritual Dynamic: Paul led the new churches immediately into the use of the gifts of the Holy Spirit (1 Cor. 12 – 14). They were not only for advanced believers. Moreover, Paul did not discourage their use just because there was imbalance. He would rather have the gifts in operation than stamp them out altogether. The church needs the supernatural gifts of the Holy Spirit until Jesus returns (1 Cor. 1:7)!

21 but test everything; hold fast what is good.

test everything

Test the supernatural things that happen (1 Cor. 14:29). Some of it is of God. A lot of it is of the flesh out of immaturity. Occasionally there may also be some demonic activity.

Paul does not say here exactly how to test what is happening. We can test the gifts in several ways. Do they build up the church, rather than tear down (1 Cor. 12:7; 14:26)? Are the utterances biblically sound (Gal. 1:8-9; 1 John 4:1-3)? Do the prophetic words exalt the Lord Jesus (1 Cor. 12:3)? Do the prophetic words come to pass (Deut. 18:21-22)? Is there character and accountability in the life of the prophet (Matt. 7:15-20)?

hold fast what is good

Encourage the gifts to be exercised but do so with discernment, looking for what is good and not just what is bad.

In spite of the abuse of the gifts of the Spirit, Paul's own deep appreciation for the central role of the Holy Spirit in the life of the church will not allow for correcting abuse by commanding disuse. The solution for abuse is proper use. Paul does the same thing in 1

Corinthians 12 – 14, where he begins with affirmation of the gifts, corrects some abuses and then ends very positively with "earnestly desire to prophesy, and do not forbid speaking in tongues. But all things should be done decently and in order" (1 Cor. 14:39-40).

22 Abstain from every form of evil.

every form of evil

The King James translation is: "Abstain from all appearance of evil." Consequently, this is the common application of this verse by many Christians today – that they should avoid even the appearance of evil. Often that is appropriate, although Jesus Himself did not always do that and neither did Paul. Paul's command here is to avoid every "kind" of evil – the focus is not just on appearances.

Further, while we should abstain from every kind of evil, this statement probably should be connected with the previous three verses regarding the work of the Holy Spirit.

In verses 19-20, Paul warns against a deliberate suppression of the moving of the Holy Spirit in the church. Sadly, that happens in many churches today. Often it happens because the church leaders have seen so much abuse that they end up despising the exercise of the spiritual gifts (verse 20). Therefore, we must work hard at testing what happens (verse 21). We must hold fast to what is good (verse 21) and reject everything that is not (verse 22). God has given us His Holy Spirit and His gifts to build up the Body (1 Cor. 12:7) – we need Him and His work!

5:23-24 GOD'S EMPOWERING

23 Now may the God of peace Himself sanctify you completely, and may your whole spirit and soul and body be kept blameless at the coming of our Lord Jesus Christ.

the God of peace

Paul, perhaps from his Jewish heritage (where *shalom* was the common greeting), makes "peace" the language of his prayer – wholeness (Rom. 15:33; 16:20; Phil. 4:9; Heb. 13:20; 2 Thess. 3:16). This wholeness is then expressed in the rest of the verse.

Elsewhere, Paul uses the expressions "God of hope" (Rom. 15:13) and "God of love and peace" (2 Cor. 13:11).

completely

The Christian life is a process. By the work of the Holy Spirit, we are in a lifelong, continual process of transformation "from one degree of glory to another," and our ultimate goal is the image of the Lord Jesus in us (2 Cor. 3:18).

Himself

Emphasizes that God Himself will do this. We cannot do this by our own strength (John 15:5), but He can and He will do it!

whole spirit and soul and body

This is the classic proof-text for the popular idea that man has three "parts" – spirit, soul and body. Biblically that doctrine is not sound. Man is a unity.

The Hebrew word for soul (נֶפֶשׁ, *nephesh*) occurs more than 700 times in the Old Testament and is translated variously as "soul," "life, "person," etc. The soul, or *nephesh*, is not, as is commonly believed, some part of you consisting of the mind, emotions and will.[35] The Bible teaches not that man has a soul, but that man is a soul: "and man became a living soul" (Gen. 2:7). In its most common usage, *nephesh* (or soul) means the "man himself," the "individual" or the "person." The soul is the person, not a part of him. *Nephesh* can also mean "life" in a general sense (e.g., Ex. 21:23).

Usually, however, *nephesh* means the person as a whole. "All the persons (*nephesh*) of the house of Jacob who came into Egypt were seventy." (Gen. 46:27) The word occurs in other Semitic languages and dialects, and means person and life too.

The New Testament is written in the context of the Old Testament, and "soul" has the same meaning in both Testaments. The Greek word for soul is ψυχή *(psyché)*. It means the person himself in many New Testament passages (e.g., Matt. 26:38). *Psyché* is also used to mean "life" in the New Testament, and is correctly translated that way in many passages (e.g., Acts 15:26).

There is a sense in which "soul" is used, although rarely, in both Testaments for the immaterial, spiritual aspect of man, in contrast to his body;[36] but even then the "soul" is seen to be incomplete without the body, and a state of separation between body and "soul" is considered to be both unnatural and temporary (2 Cor. 5:1-4).

---

35   The idea of a "tripartite soul" originated with Plato who taught that the soul consists of the *logos* (mind), the *thymos* (emotions) and *eros* (appetites or desires).
36   E.g., 1 Kings 17:21-22; Is. 10:18; Matt. 10:28; Rev. 6:9; 20:4.

Man is a unity. God created man as a unity and He intended man to remain a unity forever. But man sinned and incurred physical death (the dissolution of the body, and the separation of the soul, or person, from the body), and that is why the Gospel of redemption is the Gospel of the resurrection of the body (1 Cor. 15) and the restoration of the unity, completeness and wholeness of man as God had created him.

It's extraordinary that the doctrine of man as a tripartite being is believed by Christians all over the world, yet is based upon this one statement here!

In reality, Paul is not trying to establish a major abstract, theoretical, complicated doctrine about the nature of man in his closing words at the end of his letter to the newly-saved Thessalonian church.[37] Instead, he is blessing them. His words essentially mean, "May God bless you completely!" "May God keep you and bless you through and through!" The blessing here is similar in nature to Paul's final blessing in 2 Thessalonians 3:16: "Now may the Lord of peace Himself give you peace at all times in every way ... "

Likewise, when Jesus taught us to "love the Lord your God with all your heart and with all your soul and with all your mind and with all your strength" in Mark 12:30, He was not establishing a new doctrine that man has four parts! He was commanding us to love God with all our being!

---

[37] Paul's teaching is never abstract and theoretical whether he addresses new believers or mature believers. His teaching is always practical. Moreover, it is impossible for us to understand the nature of man, any more than we can comprehend the infinite nature of God. Man is simply far too complex. So Paul never even attempts to do that; instead his practical teaching shows us how to live to know God and glorify Him. In this way, Paul was completely unlike the pagan Greek philosophers of his time who constructed detailed analyses, dividing the soul into two (Cicero), three (Plato, Philo) or even eight (Stoics) components. When scholars today insist on doing the same kind of abstract, theoretical analysis they expose the pagan Greek origins of their mindset.

> **Instructional Dynamic:** Healthy teaching is practical teaching. This is how Jesus and all the other leaders and teachers in the New Testament taught. They were not Greeks, obsessing over complicated abstractions. Everything they taught was to build life (1 Cor. 2:1-5; 1 Tim. 1:3-5)!

blameless at the coming of our Lord Jesus Christ

The Bride of Christ, spotless and without blemish before her Lord at His return (Eph. 5:27).

24 He who calls you is faithful; He will surely do it.

faithful

God is faithful and He will surely protect you and finish the work He has begun in you (John 10:27-29; Phil. 1:6; 2 Thess. 3:3). Trust Him! He is one who builds your life and who builds His church! It is His work; trust Him.

5:25-28 FINAL INSTRUCTIONS AND BLESSING

25 Brothers, pray for us.

Brothers

The whole church is to pray for Paul, not just the intercessors. As he prayed constantly for them (1 Thess. 1:2), they must also pray for him.

Paul frequently requests prayer (Rom. 15:30-32; 2 Cor. 1:11; Eph. 6:18-20; Phil. 1:19; Col. 4:3-4; 2 Thess. 3:1-3; Phm. 22; Heb. 13:18-19). He knew its power!

> **Spiritual Dynamic:** The work of church planting and building is a spiritual one. It is the work of the Holy Spirit, and not man's organizational ability. Healthy churches are born and mature through travail and prayer.

26 Greet all the brothers with a holy kiss.

all the brothers

Remarkably, within the believing community this love is between everyone: rich and poor, slave and free, Jew and Gentile!

Love is the outer garment in which everything in the Body of Christ is wrapped.

holy kiss

Holy, not sensuous, in form, expressing Christian love rather than romantic love (Rom. 16:16; 1 Cor. 16:20; 2 Cor. 13:12; 1 Pet. 5:14). Kissing on the cheek was a common form of greeting in many countries in Paul's day as it is today. By promoting this practice, Paul was encouraging an outward physical expression of true Christian love and affection in a form that was culturally acceptable and appropriate.

27 I put you under oath before the Lord to have this letter read to all the brothers.

under oath before the Lord

This is a very serious charge! This letter absolutely must be read to everyone.

Paul's strong words may indicate a suspicion on Paul's part that someone else was using or might use his name and authority to spread false teaching (see 2 Thess. 2:2). 2 Thessalonians 3:17 expresses a similar concern to authenticate his letter.

> **Instructional Dynamic:** Without the teaching of the truth, the church will be weak and exposed to mortal danger. The leaders must teach the truth and also protect the people from errors.

have this letter read

Many people could not read, so reading this letter aloud was the only way everyone could receive it (Col. 4:16).

Every Member Functions: Paul wrote for the church as a whole and wanted everyone to hear his instructions. Thus, all the instructions in this letter are for everyone, not just the leaders. There is no clergy-laity distinction in Paul's mind. In a healthy church, the people do the work of the ministry; they are not merely passive recipients of ministry done by someone else for their benefit.

28 *The grace of our Lord Jesus Christ be with you.*

The grace of our Lord Jesus Christ

In Paul's final blessing he closes the letter as he began it – with God's grace given to us through union with Christ.

1 Thessalonians and the Healthy Church Model

In many ways, 1 Thessalonians provides us with a manual for planting and building churches.

When examining the letter through the lens of the Healthy Church Model[38] it becomes very clear and practical exactly how to plant and build a church.

THE GOAL OF CHURCH LIFE

First, the Healthy Church Model gives a clear goal for church life, describing the seven areas in which a church needs to be healthy:

1. Christ is central and preeminent in everything. Every member experiences union with Him, with all that is in their life and ministry coming from that.
2. Every member functions.
3. Every member loves God, obeys Him and grows in Him.
4. Every member loves others and serves them.
5. Every member builds others.
6. Every member reaches out to the lost.

---

38 Please see *Building Healthy Churches* by Malcolm Webber.

7. The local church has healthy relationships with the wider church, in the fellowship of the Holy Spirit.

Here are just a few of the passages in 1 Thessalonians that refer to each of these seven things. There are many more. It would be a good exercise to go through the letter and find every passage that refers to each one.

1. **Christ is central and preeminent in everything. Every member experiences union with Him with everything in their life and ministry coming from that.**

   For we know, brothers loved by God, that He has chosen you, (1 Thess. 1:4)

   Now may our God and Father Himself, and our Lord Jesus, direct our way to you, and may the Lord make you increase and abound in love for one another and for all, as we do for you, so that He may establish your hearts blameless in holiness before our God and Father, at the coming of our Lord Jesus with all His saints. (1 Thess. 3:11-13)

   Now may the God of peace Himself sanctify you completely, and may your whole spirit and soul and body be kept blameless at the coming of our Lord Jesus Christ. He who calls you is faithful; He will surely do it. (1 Thess. 5:23-24)

2. **Every member functions.**

   The entire letter is addressed to all the believers at Thessalonica. Paul repeatedly affirms them in all they're doing and expresses his desire for all of them to do it more.

   We give thanks to God always for all of you, constantly mentioning you in our prayers, remembering before our God and Father your work of faith and labor of love and steadfastness of hope in our Lord Jesus Christ. (1 Thess. 1:2-3)

we exhorted each one of you and encouraged you and charged you to walk in a manner worthy of God, who calls you into his own kingdom and glory. (1 Thess. 2:12)

as we pray most earnestly night and day that we may see you face to face and supply what is lacking in your faith ... (1 Thess. 3:10)

For you are all children of light, children of the day. We are not of the night or of the darkness. (1 Thess. 5:5)

3. **Every member loves God, obeys Him and grows in Him.**

    remembering before our God and Father your work of faith and labor of love and steadfastness of hope in our Lord Jesus Christ. (1 Thess. 1:3)

    so that He may establish your hearts blameless in holiness before our God and Father, at the coming of our Lord Jesus with all His saints. (1 Thess. 3:13)

    For this is the will of God, your sanctification: that you abstain from sexual immorality; that each one of you know how to control his own body in holiness and honor, (1 Thess. 4:3-5)

    Rejoice always, pray without ceasing, give thanks in all circumstances; for this is the will of God in Christ Jesus for you. (1 Thess. 5:16-18)

    Abstain from every form of evil. (1 Thess. 5:22)

4. **Every member loves others and serves them.**

    and may the Lord make you increase and abound in love for one another and for all, as we do for you, (1 Thess. 3:12)

    Now concerning brotherly love you have no need for anyone to write to you, for you yourselves have been taught by God to love one another, for that indeed is what you are doing to all the brothers throughout Macedonia. But we urge you, brothers, to do this more and more, (1 Thess. 4:9-10)

See that no one repays anyone evil for evil, but always seek to do good to one another and to everyone. (1 Thess. 5:15)

Greet all the brothers with a holy kiss. (1 Thess. 5:26)

5. **Every member builds others.**

    Therefore encourage one another with these words. (1 Thess. 4:18)

    Therefore encourage one another and build one another up, just as you are doing. (1 Thess. 5:11)

    And we urge you, brothers, admonish the idle, encourage the fainthearted, help the weak, be patient with them all. (1 Thess. 5:14)

6. **Every member reaches out to the lost.**

    For not only has the Word of the Lord sounded forth from you in Macedonia and Achaia, but your faith in God has gone forth everywhere, so that we need not say anything. (1 Thess. 1:8)

    and may the Lord make you increase and abound in love for one another and for all, as we do for you, (1 Thess. 3:12)

    so that you may walk properly before outsiders … (1 Thess. 4:12)

    See that no one repays anyone evil for evil, but always seek to do good to one another and to everyone. (1 Thess. 5:15)

7. **The local church has healthy relationships with the wider church, in the fellowship of the Holy Spirit.**

    so that you became an example to all the believers in Macedonia and in Achaia. (1 Thess. 1:7)

    Now concerning brotherly love you have no need for anyone to write to you, for you yourselves have been taught by God to love one another, for that indeed is what you are doing to all the brothers throughout Macedonia. But we urge you, brothers, to do this more and more, (1 Thess. 4:9-10)

THE PROCESS OF CHURCH LIFE

Second, the Healthy Church Model shows us a clear process in which a church will be planted and then built. These are the Four Dynamics of Transformation:

1. Spiritual Dynamics – including prayer, worship, reflection, meditation in the Word.
2. Relational Dynamics – including encouragement, affirmation, accountability, correction, examples, mentors, coaches.
3. Experiential Dynamics – including obedience, learning by doing, challenging assignments, and pressure.
4. Instructional Dynamics – the teaching of the Word of God in an engaging and interactive way, integrating doctrine into the context of life, experiences and relationships

Here are a few of the passages in 1 Thessalonians that refer to each of the four:

1. **Spiritual Dynamic:**

Paul originally came to Macedonia in response to a direct revelation from God (Acts 16:9-10).

> *We give thanks to God always for all of you, constantly mentioning you in our prayers, (1 Thess. 1:2)*

> *because our Gospel came to you not only in Word, but also in power and in the Holy Spirit and with full conviction ... (1 Thess. 1:5)*

> *... you received the Word in much affliction, with the joy of the Holy Spirit, (1 Thess. 1:6)*

> *Now may our God and Father Himself, and our Lord Jesus, direct our way to you, (1 Thess. 3:11)*
>
> *pray without ceasing (1 Thess. 5:17)*
>
> *Do not despise prophecies, but test everything; hold fast what is good. Abstain from every form of evil. (1 Thess. 5:2–22)*
>
> *Brothers, pray for us. (1 Thess. 5:25)*

2. **Relational Dynamic:**

Paul frequently used the term, "as you know." The Thessalonians knew him deeply!

> *… You know what kind of men we proved to be among you for your sake. (1 Thess. 1:5)*
>
> *But we were gentle among you, like a nursing mother taking care of her own children. So, being affectionately desirous of you, we were ready to share with you not only the Gospel of God but also our own selves, because you had become very dear to us. (1 Thess. 1:7-8)*
>
> *You are witnesses, and God also, how holy and righteous and blameless was our conduct toward you believers. For you know how, like a father with his children, we exhorted each one of you and encouraged you and charged you to walk in a manner worthy of God, who calls you into His own Kingdom and glory. (1 Thess. 1:10-12)*
>
> *Nor did we seek glory from people, whether from you or from others, though we could have made demands as apostles of Christ. But we were gentle among you, like a nursing mother taking care of her own children. So, being affectionately desirous of you, we were ready to share with you not only the Gospel of God but also our own selves, because you had become very dear to us. For you remember, brothers, our labor and toil: we worked night and day, that we might not be a burden to any of you, while we proclaimed to you the Gospel of God. You are witnesses, and God also, how holy and righteous and blameless was our conduct toward you believers.*

> *For you know how, like a father with his children, we exhorted each one of you and encouraged you and charged you to walk in a manner worthy of God, who calls you into His own Kingdom and glory. (1 Thess. 2:6-12)*

> *For what is our hope or joy or crown of boasting before our Lord Jesus at His coming? Is it not you? For you are our glory and joy. (1 Thess. 2:19-20)*

> *… you always remember us kindly and long to see us, as we long to see you (1 Thess. 3:6)*

3. **Experiential Dynamic:**

> *And you became imitators of us and of the Lord, for you received the Word in much affliction, with the joy of the Holy Spirit, (1 Thess. 1:6)*

> *… you turned to God from idols to serve the living and true God, (1 Thess. 1:9)*

> *And we also thank God constantly for this, that when you received the Word of God, which you heard from us, you accepted it not as the word of men but as what it really is, the Word of God, which is at work in you believers. For you, brothers, became imitators of the churches of God in Christ Jesus that are in Judea. For you suffered the same things from your own countrymen as they did from the Jews, (1 Thess. 1:13-14)*

> *we exhorted each one of you and encouraged you and charged you to walk in a manner worthy of God, who calls you into His own Kingdom and glory. (1 Thess. 2:12)*

> *Finally, then, brothers, we ask and urge you in the Lord Jesus, that as you received from us how you ought to walk and to please God, just as you are doing, that you do so more and more. (1 Thess. 4:1)*

4. **Instructional Dynamic:**

Most of the Thessalonian believers were Gentiles (1 Thess. 1:9; 2:15). They had no prior knowledge of God or of the Old Testament Scriptures. This church essentially started from "zero." Thus, Paul had to teach them everything. He would have chosen very carefully what he did teach them – the foundational things of God.

Paul's teaching wove through the spiritual, relational and experiential context. Moreover, he tells us what he taught them. Apparently, these are the significant things to teach a new church:

- The church (1:1)
- The triune Godhead (1:1)
- The grace of God (1:1)
- Prayer (1:2)
- Salvation by faith (1:3)
- Love one another in deed (1:3)
- Union with Christ (1:3)
- The wider Body of Christ (1:7)
- Sharing their faith with others (1:8)
- Turning from idolatry (1:9)
- Jesus' death and resurrection (1:10)
- The soon return of the Lord Jesus (1:10; 4:16)
- God's eternal judgment of sinners (1:10)
- Persecution (2:2)
- Fivefold ministry (2:6)
- Spiritual authority and servant leadership (2:6-12)
- Righteous lifestyle (2:12)
- Kingdom of God (2:12)
- Authority of the Word of God (2:13)
- Jesus' life and death (2:15)
- The prophets of the Old Testament (2:15)
- The Great Commission (2:16)
- Satan and spiritual warfare (2:18)
- Eternal rewards (2:19)
- Sufferings (3:4)
- Temptation (3:5)
- Sovereignty of God (3:11)
- Love toward all men (3:12)

- Holiness (3:13)
- Sexual purity (4:2-8)
- The gift of the Holy Spirit (4:8)
- Personal financial responsibility (4:11)
- Life after death (4:13)
- Resurrection of the body (4:16)
- The Day of the Lord (5:2-3)
- Holy lifestyle (5:5-8)
- Leadership (5:12-13)
- Forgiveness of others (5:15)
- Generosity (5:15)
- Spiritual gifts (5:19-22)
- Sanctification (5:23)
- God's faithfulness (5:24)

At first glance, this may look like a lot of teaching, but remember that Paul did not teach long courses or classes as we do. He simply brought up the appropriate instruction at the appropriate time. Like Jesus' teaching, Paul's would have been given in relatively short pieces, dealing with the main issues.

Paul's teaching was always practical, not abstract or theoretical. It was the clear Word of God, not the ideas or traditions of man. He taught the core truths of the Scripture, not peripheral or unclear doctrines.

Moreover, his teaching was always empowered by the Holy Spirit. This teaching brought life and fruitfulness to the new church, and laid a strong foundation for their powerful growth and impact.

www.ingramcontent.com/pod-product-compliance
Lightning Source LLC
LaVergne TN
LVHW051837080426
835512LV00018B/2926